EXAM *Revision*

AQA(A) A2

Psychology

Jean-Marc Lawton

To Mara, without whom the sky would fall in.

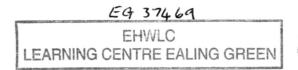

Philip Allan Updates, an imprint of Hodder Education, an Hachette UK company, Market Place, Deddington, Oxfordshire OX15 0SE

Orders
Bookpoint Ltd, 130 Milton Park, Abingdon, Oxfordshire OX14 4SB
tel: 01235 827720
fax: 01235 400454
e-mail: uk.orders@bookpoint.co.uk
Lines are open 9.00 a.m.–5.00 p.m., Monday to Saturday, with a 24-hour message answering service.
You can also order through the Philip Allan Updates website: www.philipallan.co.uk

© Philip Allan Updates 2010
ISBN 978-0-340-98750-6

First printed 2010

Impression number	5	4	3	2	1
Year	2014	2013	2012	2011	2010

Printed in Spain

Environmental information
Hachette UK's policy is to use papers that are natural, renewable and recyclable products and made from wood grown in sustainable forests. The logging and manufacturing processes are expected to conform to the environmental regulations of the country of origin.

Contents

Introduction v

Unit 3 Topics in psychology

Topic 1 Biological rhythms and sleep

A Biological rhythms 2
B Sleep states 4
C Disorders of sleep 7

Topic 2 Perception

A Theories of perceptual organisation 10
B Development of perception 12
C Face recognition and visual agnosias 16

Topic 3 Relationships

A The formation, maintenance and breakdown of romantic relationships ... 19
B Human reproductive behaviour 22
C Effects of early experience and culture on adult relationships 25

Topic 4 Aggression

A Social psychological approaches to explaining aggression 28
B Biological approaches to explaining aggression 31
C Aggression as an adaptive response 33

Topic 5 Eating behaviour

A Eating behaviour 37
B Biological explanations of eating behaviour 40
C Eating disorders 42

Topic 6 Gender

A Psychological explanations of gender development 46
B Biological influences on gender 49
C Social contexts of gender role 51

Topic 7 Intelligence and learning

A Theories of intelligence 54
B Animal learning and intelligence 57
C Evolution and intelligence 60

Topic 8 Cognition and development

A Development of thinking 64
B Development of moral understanding 68
C Development of social cognition 70

Unit 4 Psychopathology, psychology in action and research methods

Topic 9   Psychopathology

   A Schizophrenia 74
   B Depression 81
   C Anxiety disorders 89

Topic 10   Psychology in action

   A Media psychology 102
   B The psychology of addictive behaviour 111
   C Anomalistic psychology 119

Topic 11   Psychological research and scientific method

   A The application of scientific method in psychology 128
   B Designing psychological investigations 130
   C Data analysis and reporting on investigations 133

Introduction

About this book

This book will provide you with the guidance and focus you need to do well in AQA (A) A2 examinations.

These are exam revision notes. It is worth considering the implications of this. The fact it is concerned with exam preparation is important. It is likely you will be making most use of this book in the build-up to the exams themselves (rather than as you write class essays or do mock exams). However, many students take modular rather than terminal exam courses. This book serves the needs of both groups, though they will use it in different ways: modular students will use it throughout their course, whereas terminal exam students may only get involved with it in the last couple of terms.

The word 'revision' triggers a key assumption made about you. The word literally means 'to see again'. In other words, the topics, concepts, theories and studies should be familiar to you from textbooks, school/college classes, and wider reading. Clearly this book serves a different function from a textbook and can only point you in the right directions. So if in order to understand topic X you need to be familiar with theory Y and study Z, you will need to ensure you know them in detail. It is only possible to give thumbnail sketches and summarise main points and findings. This is reflected in the final word in the title: 'notes'. The bullet-point approach, free of dense text, will help you see through to the bare bones of what you need to know. It is then for you to elaborate on this.

What you will find here is a list of the things you need to know and the things you need to be able to do. Any book can only do so much. It is for you to make it 'come alive'. By this it is meant that you should endeavour to make it interactive: innumerable psychological studies have shown that active learning is superior to passive learning. Think carefully about the specimen questions. It will be time well spent. Look up things which are unfamiliar. Make your own notes and read critically (ask yourself why a particular finding is important, why a particular study is relevant to answering a specific question) — never just let the words drift past your eyes!

Please do not turn the pages expecting to see a set of the 'right' answers to questions. Most examiners get alarmed if they hear students are trying to rote-learn model answers. There are at least two good reasons for this. First, psychology is not the kind of discipline where there is just one right answer — it is not like mathematics. Second, an answer only earns marks insofar as it answers the question on the exam paper. Just a slight change of wording requires a change in the balance and content of the answer.

Throughout the book you will find reference to 'names and dates', such as 'Zigler and Phillips (1961) believed that...'. This is a standard academic convention, giving authority to what you are writing (rather than 'I think that...'), and shows that you are giving a source for an experiment, a definition, etc. Do not worry about remembering them all; just do the best you can. If you can include some, it will impress the examiners, but they will not knock marks off if you cannot. They are included as it is the recognised way of writing in psychology and to give you the opportunity to use them where you can and to be able to find them in your textbooks.

The book is specifically written to the AQA (A) A2 specification. Although students taking other examinations will find much of interest here, focus is specifically on the one examination, so students taking it will not have to wade through volumes of material with no relevance or use to them, and have uncertainties about which sections are relevant and which are not. If you are taking the AQA (A) A2 exams, everything in this book is relevant to you.

It is assumed that you want to succeed in your exams. This is presumably why you have bought the book. We are talking attitude here, and attitude is half the battle. As sports coaches say, 'No pain, no gain.' The book is, hopefully, easy to read and as enjoyable as any revision guide can be, but the rest is down to you.

The A2 examinations

The AQA (A) A2 specification is divided into two units, each with different topic areas:

- Unit 3: biological rhythms and sleep, perception, relationships, aggression, eating behaviour, gender, intelligence and learning, and cognition and development.
- Unit 4: psychopathology, psychology in action and research methods.

As you prepare for the examination, you need to have covered the material listed in the specification (your teacher will have a copy of this). The questions set in the exams may sample the whole range of the specification. In Unit 3, for example, 'perception' is divided into three parts: theories of perceptual organisation; development of perception; and face recognition and visual agnosias. If the specification names a particular theory (for example, 'Gibson's top-down/indirect theory' and an alternative, such as Gibson's bottom-up/direct theory', then you must cover these as they can be specifically included in Unit 3 questions.

Assessment objectives

Units 3 and 4 are assessed through three skills, called assessment objective 1 (AO1 for short), assessment objective 2 (AO2) and assessment objective 3 (AO3).

Assessment objective 1

Quite simply, AO1 requires clear and effective communication of your knowledge and understanding of a particular topic. Knowledge and understanding are essentially descriptive: for example, a demonstration that you know the main features of Gibson's theory of perception. This is like retelling the story line of a film you have seen.

For AO1, candidates should be able to:

- recognise, recall and show understanding of knowledge
- select, organise and communicate relevant information in a variety of forms

Assessment objective 2

AO2 requires application of knowledge and understanding of a particular topic. Application of knowledge is like adding commentary (this part of the film worked well because...). This mainly involves analysis and evaluation; analysis is taking things (such as a theory) apart and looking at the constituent elements, and evaluation is an appraisal of their worth (what are the good features of the theory and what are its weaknesses?).

For AO2, candidates should be able to:

- analyse and evaluate knowledge and processes
- apply knowledge and processes to unfamiliar situations, including those relating to issues
- assess the validity, reliability and credibility of information

Assessment objective 3

AO3 concerns how science works with regard to psychology. This requires both knowledge of research methodology and the ability to analyse and evaluate such knowledge.

For AO3, candidates should be able to:

- describe ethical, safe and skilful practical techniques and processes, selecting appropriate qualitative and quantitative methods
- know how to make, record and communicate reliable and valid observations and measurements with appropriate accuracy and precision, through using primary and secondary sources
- analyse, interpret, explain and evaluate the methodology, results and impact of their own and others' experimental and investigative activities in a variety of ways

The structure of the questions

All of the questions assessing Units 3 and 4 are set to a particular formula.

Unit 3 is divided into eight sections: Biological rhythms and sleep; Perception; Relationships; Aggression; Eating behaviour; Gender; Intelligence and learning; and Cognition and development.

This paper accounts for 50 % of the total A2 marks and 25 % of the total A-level (AS + A2).

There will be one question on each of the eight topics. You must answer three of these questions. These can take the form of essay questions or parted essay questions which will assess AO1, AO2 and AO3 skills. Examples of these types of question are included within each topic section of this revision book

Each question is worth 25 marks, comprising 9 AO1 marks, 12 AO2 marks and 4 AO3 marks. This means there are 75 marks available in total for this paper, comprising 27 AO1 marks, 36 AO2 marks and 12 AO3 marks.

You may sit this paper in either January or June.

Unit 4 is divided into three sections: Psychopathology; Psychology in action; and Research methods.

This paper accounts for 50 % of the total A2 marks and 25 % of the total A-level (AS + A2).

The 'Psychopathology' section of the examination contains three questions, one on each of the three subsections: Schizophrenia; Depression; and Anxiety disorders, of which you must answer one question. This section totals 25 marks, comprising 9 AO1 marks, 12 AO2 marks and 4 AO3 marks.

The 'Psychology in action' section of the examination contains three questions, one on each of the three subsections: Media psychology; The psychology of addictive behaviour; and Anomalistic psychology, of which you must answer one question. This section totals 25 marks, comprising 9 AO1 marks, 12 AO2 marks and 4 AO3 marks.

On both the 'Psychopathology' and 'Psychology in action' sections, questions can take the form of essay questions or parted essay questions. Examples of these types of question are included within each topic section of this revision book.

The 'Research methods' section of the examination contains one structured question divided into sub-questions, based upon some stimulus material. All parts of this question must be answered. This section totals 35 marks, comprising 3 AO1 marks, 4 AO2 marks and 28 AO3 marks.

This means there are 85 marks available in total for this paper, comprising 21 AO1 marks, 28 AO2 marks and 36 AO3 marks.

You may sit this paper in either January or June.

Command words

Command words are the words used in questions to instruct you what kind of answer is needed. By having an understanding of these terms, you will be more able to create answers in line with what each individual question requires, so you can gain the maximum amount of marks on offer.

Here is a list of common examination injunctions with a brief explanation of what each one requires.

AO1 command words
Identify = name
Name = identify
Define = what is meant by
Outline = give brief details without explanation
Describe = give a detailed account without explanation

AO2 command words
Analyse = examine in detail
Give = show awareness of

Explain = give a clear account of why and how something is so
Evaluate = assess the value or effectiveness
Discuss = give a reasoned balanced, account
Apply = explain how something can be used

AO3 command words
Outline = give brief details without explanation
Give = show awareness of
Identify = name
Explain = give a clear account of why and how something is so
Write = compose your own example

How much should I aim to write?

In Unit test 3 you have to answer your selected questions in 90 minutes, while in Unit test 4 you have 2 hours to answer your selected questions and the compulsory research methods question. Allowing essential time for reading the questions, making choices, planning answers and checking through for mistakes, you will probably have less than this as actual writing time.

A good revision strategy is to practise writing answers to exam-style questions. (Indeed, it is recommended that you adopt this practice throughout your course and not just as a final revision strategy.) There are a number of exam-style questions available to look at on the AQA website. It is also a good idea to look at how many marks are available for parted questions; this provides a rough guide as to how much to write. If you practise answering questions enough, you will become skilled at providing enough material in the time available to give yourself access to the full range of marks on offer. Remember not to write too much, as that will waste valuable time that you could have spent on another question, or on another part of a question. You do not have to write everything you know on a topic, merely sufficient to gain access to all the marks. Once you have earned all the marks available for a particular question, or a particular part of a question, then writing any more will not gain extra credit, however good the material is. If you do this, you are reducing the amount of time available to you to attempt the other questions on the paper.

There is a wealth of exam-style questions provided throughout this book that you can utilise as part of your studies and also for final revision before you sit your exams.

How will my work be marked?

On the 'Research methods' section of the Unit 4 test, questions requiring shorter answers generally gain initial marks for providing accurate answers, with any additional marks available being awarded for the degree of elaboration given.

For longer answer questions, mark bands are used to assess students' answers. Examples of mark schemes can be found on the AQA website in the sample questions and mark schemes section (see **www.aqa.org.uk**).

The AS exam

The AS is the first half of the A-level qualification. Your final grade will be determined by simply adding together your AS and A2 scores. So it is possible, though not advisable, to fail the AS, but still pass the A-level (e.g. fail the AS by 5 marks but pass the A2 by 6). So never give up!

Unit 3
Topics in Psychology

A Biological rhythms

1 Circadian, infradian and ultradian rhythms

Biological rhythms are behaviours occurring in cycles, controlled either by *endogenous pacemakers* (internal biological clocks regulating biological functioning) or by *exogenous zeitgebers* (external/ environmental cues, such as seasonal changes).

Circadian rhythms. These are biological cycles lasting around 24 hours, such as the sleep/wake cycle. There is a free-running cycle controlled by an endogenous pacemaker working as a 'body clock'. Another circadian rhythm is *body temperature*, rising and falling as an indicator of metabolic rate.

Siffre (1972) spent 6 months in a cave with no time cues, settling into a sleep/wake cycle of 25–30 hours, while **Aschoff and Weber (1965)** found that participants in a bunker with no natural light settled into a sleep/wake cycle of 25–27 hours, implying that endogenous pacemakers exert a strong influence on circadian rhythms.

- Isolation studies have few participants, making generalisation problematic, although research suggests that endogenous pacemakers exist and are regulated by exogenous zeitgebers.
- Practical applications include designing timetables around optimal times to study/work, or when best to take medicines.

Infradian rhythms. These are biological cycles lasting more than 24 hours, such as the menstrual cycle, controlled by the hypothalamus acting as an endogenous pacemaker, with exogenous zeitgebers playing a part too. Infradian rhythms include *circannual rhythms* occurring once a year, such as hibernation.

Russell et al. (1980) applied donors' underarm sweat to upper lips of female participants, finding that menstrual cycles became synchronised. This suggests that pheromones act as exogenous zeitgebers.

McClintock and Stern (1998) found that pheromones in donors' sweat affected recipients' menstrual cycles, suggesting that exogenous zeitgebers have a regulating effect.

- Synchronised periods may have evolutionary significance in allowing women living together to synchronise pregnancies and share child-caring duties.
- Women working in proximity to men have shorter cycles, bestowing an evolutionary advantage in giving more opportunities to get pregnant.

Ultradian rhythms. These are biological cycles lasting less than 24 hours, such as the cycle of brain activity during sleep. Sleep has several stages through the night, lasting for about an hour in infancy to 90 minutes by adolescence.

Rechtschaffen and Kales (1968) measured electrical activity of the brain, finding different patterns of activity at different times of sleep.

Gerkema and Dann (1985) found ultradian rhythms to be correlated with brain and body size, with larger animals having longer cycles.

- Lesions to brain areas controlling circadian rhythms have no effect on behaviours with ultradian rhythms, suggesting that circadian and ultradian rhythms have different controlling mechanisms.

- Much research into ultradian rhythms involves animals, creating problems with generalising to humans.

Role of endogenous pacemakers. The main pacemaker is the superchiasmatic nucleus (SCN), a small group of cells in the hypothalamus generating a circadian rhythm reset by light entering the eyes. A rhythm is produced from the interaction of proteins, producing a biological clock.

> **Hawkins and Armstrong-Esther (1978)** found that shift-work altered nurses' sleep–wake cycles, but not temperature cycles, suggesting that different body clocks regulate different circadian rhythms.
>
> **Morgan (1995)** found that removing SCN cells from hamsters made circadian rhythms disappear, but that they returned when cells were transplanted in, showing the role of the SCN as an endogenous pacemaker.

- There is an adaptive advantage in animals having endogenous pacemakers reset by exogenous zeitgebers, keeping them in tune with seasonal changes, day/night changes, etc.

Role of exogenous zeitgebers. Zeitgebers help to reset biological rhythms and endogenous pacemakers respond to zeitgebers, coordinating behaviours regulated with external environments. Light, weather patterns and food availability are important zeitgebers.

> **Klein et al. (1993)** found that a blind man with a circadian rhythm of 24.5 hours got out of synchronisation with the 24-hour day. He took medication to regulate his sleep–wake cycle. This suggests that light acts as an exogenous time cue.

- Relying solely upon exogenous zeitgebers could threaten survival, therefore internal cues are important too.

Q (a) Describe what is meant by endogenous pacemakers and exogenous zeitgebers. *(9 marks)*

(b) Assess the consequences of disrupting circadian rhythms. *(16 marks)*

2 Consequences of disrupting biological rhythms

Usually exogenous zeitgebers change gradually, giving time to adjust. However, rapid change disrupts coordination between internally regulated rhythms and external exogenous zeitgebers, creating consequences for the ability to function properly.

Jet lag. This is caused by travelling across time zones so quickly that biological rhythms cannot match external cues, causing sleepiness during daytime and restfulness at night. This lasts until resynchronisation occurs, which is best achieved by being allowed to follow exogenous zeitgebers (e.g. stay awake until night). Jet lag is worse travelling west to east, as it is easier to adjust biological clocks if they are ahead of local time (*phase delay*) than behind (*phase advance*). Jet lag also occurs by the biological clock regulating temperature needing time to reset, causing desynchronised rhythms in the meantime.

> **Klein et al. (1972)** found that adjustment to jet lag occurred more easily on westbound flights, whether outbound or homebound, implying that phase advance has more severe consequences.
>
> **Schwartz et al. (1995)** found that eastern-based US baseball teams did better against teams in the west than vice versa, suggesting that phase advance has severer consequences. However, it may just be that eastern teams are superior.
>
> **Webb and Agnew (1971)** found that strategies for coping with jet lag include outdoor pursuits, exposure to light and regular meal times, suggesting that following exogenous zeitgebers helps address the consequences of jet lag.

- As our endogenous cycle is roughly 25 hours, it is easier to deal with phase delay than phase advance.
- Concentration levels are affected by jet lag (and shift-work), implying disruption to cognitive processes.
- Much research utilises naturalistic field studies; these are high in ecological validity, but incur many confounding variables, making the establishment of causality problematic.

Shift-work. This can involve working when normally asleep and sleeping when normally awake, causing breakdown in the coordination between internal biological clocks and external cues. Many shift-workers change working hours every week, causing disruption to routines of eating, resting etc. and an almost permanent state of desynchronisation, impairing concentration and physical performance, and increasing stress levels that incur long-term health risks.

Research shows that shift-work patterns involving phase delay — changing shifts forward in time — cause less disruption, as does an adjustment time before changing shifts.

Czeisler et al. (1982) found that shift-workers had high illness rates, sleep disorders and elevated stress levels, suggesting that internal body clocks were out of synchronisation with exogenous zeitgebers. Moving to a phase delay system of rotating shifts forward in time reduced negative effects.

Sharkey (2001) found that melatonin reduced the time required to adjust to shift-work patterns and rotations, demonstrating the effects of practical applications based on psychological knowledge.

Hawkins and Armstrong-Esther (1978) found that circadian rhythms of nurses working night shifts adjusted gradually, but the temperature body clock took longer to adjust.

- Accidents such as the Chernobyl reactor meltdown occurred due to early morning concentration and decision failures, suggesting that desynchronisation effects of working irregular hours impair performance.
- Research suggests that disrupting biological rhythms affects cognitive and emotional functioning as well as physical functioning, demonstrating the severity of consequences.
- There are large individual differences in how people are affected by shift-work (and jet lag), making generalisation difficult.
- The introduction of modern travel systems and electrical lighting may have created an environment that our evolutionary determined biology cannot cope with, leading to disruption and negative consequences.

Q Critically discuss the consequences of disrupting biological rhythms. *(25 marks)*

B Sleep states

1 *The nature of sleep*

Sleep occurs as a circadian rhythm and an ultradian cycle of separate stages and is a state of consciousness of diminished responsiveness to external stimuli.

Stage 1	A light sleep where heart rate declines and muscles relax.
Stage 2	A deeper sleep, with noticeable bursts of sleep spindles
Stage 3	Increasingly deep. Sleep spindles decline, replaced by long, slow delta waves.
Stage 4	Deep sleep. Metabolic rate is low and growth hormones are released.
REM	Eye movements are noticeable and dreaming occurs.

Stages 1 to 4 take about 1 hour, then stage 3 is re-entered, followed by stage 2 and REM sleep. After 15 minutes, stages 2, 3 and 4 re-occur in order, then another cycle begins. There are about five ultradian cycles a night, with increasingly more time spent in REM sleep. This pattern is fairly universal, though there are developmental differences.

The physiology of sleep

The brain stem has a role in key functions, such as alertness and arousal, but also controls sleep behaviour, with several hormones involved too.

The SCN reacts to levels of light, stimulating melatonin production from the pineal gland, causing the release of serotonin and allowing reticular activating system activity to lessen, bringing the onset of sleep

The release of *noradrenaline* causes the onset of REM sleep and the hormone *acetylcholine* is involved with brain activation during wakefulness and REM sleep, sometimes referred to as wakeful sleep.

Aserinsky and Kleitman (1955) woke participants during periods of rapid eye movements to find they were dreaming, indicating a relationship between dreaming and REM sleep, However, this is reliant on subjective reports.

Dement and Kleitman (1957) used electroencephalogram (EEG) readings to find that sleep consists of a sequential series of five stages, each with its own characteristics, occurring in a set pattern. Participants woken at various times reported dream activity mainly during REM sleep.

Moor-Ede and Czeisler (1984) found that sleep occurs during the low point of our temperature cycle, showing the circadian nature of sleep as part of the daily sleep–wake cycle.

- The development of EEG readings allowed an objective means of studying sleep behaviour.
- Most sleep studies occur in laboratories, with participants wearing electrodes, and may not reflect normal sleep patterns.
- As sleep has five stages, it is likely that each stage has a different function. Because REM sleep is identifiable in warm-blooded, but not cold-blooded creatures, it might be that REM sleep serves the function, by increasing brain metabolism, of keeping brain temperature at a safe level.
- Dement and Kleitman's study is not representative, involving few participants. However, similar studies show their findings to be reliable and valid.

Q Describe the nature of sleep. *(9 marks)*

2 *Functions of sleep*

Humans spend a third of their time asleep, suggesting a biological function, but psychological factors are important too. There is no best theory, all explanations having weaknesses and strengths, although good theories should explain the universal nature of sleep. There are wide variations in sleep duration, but it is generally seen as essential, with an average of between 6 and 8 hours a night.

Evolutionary explanations

These see sleep as serving some adaptive advantage and occurring through natural selection. Different species evolved different types and patterns of sleep, dealing with different environmental needs, such as predator avoidance. Sleep keeps animals dormant when activities vital for survival are not required.

Predator–prey sleep. Meddis (1979) believes that sleep evolved to keep animals hidden when usual activities, such as foraging, are not required. Therefore prey animals should sleep less, being more at risk and vigilant.

Body size. Smaller animals evolved a greater need to sleep, their metabolic rates being high and energy consumption rapid. Long periods of sleep help conserve energy stores.

Stear (2005) found that sleep saves energy and is an adaptation to ecological factors differing across species, supporting the evolutionary explanation.

Requadt (2006) reported that animals find warm, safe places to sleep, minimising energy requirements to maintain body temperature.

Siegel (2008) found less risk of injury when asleep than awake, sleep being a safety device when essential activities are not necessary.

- Predators sleep longer than prey animals, supporting the evolutionary prediction. However, prey animals are usually herbivores, needing time to graze and therefore having less time to sleep.

Restoration theory

People sleep when tired, suggesting it is a period for rejuvenation. Growth hormone is released during sleep, stimulating tissue growth and aiding protein synthesis to repair damaged tissues. Waste products are also removed.

Horne (1988) developed the core sleep model — during stage 4 and REM sleep the brain refreshes itself for the next day.

Oswald (1980) developed restoration theory — accelerated brain activity during REM sleep indicates brain restoration, while growth hormone production during stages 1 to 4 sleep indicates bodily restoration.

Horne (1988) performed a meta-analysis of sleep deprivation studies, finding little evidence of reduced physical functioning or stress responses. This suggests that sleep is not primarily for restoration

Stern and Morgane (1974) believe that during REM sleep, neurotransmitter levels are replenished, supporting the restoration theory. This is backed up by the fact that anti-depressants increase neurotransmitter levels, reducing REM activity.

- Endurance athletes use naps after training to promote protein synthesis that repairs tissues, supporting the restoration theory.
- Infants sleep lots, possibly because of rapid brain and body growth, again supporting restoration theory.
- Sufferers of fatal familial insomnia cannot sleep and usually die within 2 years, implying support for the restoration theory, but cases are few and sufferers also have brain damage that may be responsible.

Q   Describe and evaluate two theories of the function of sleep.   *(25 marks)*

3   *Lifespan changes*

There are differences in how much sleep individuals need, but there are important developmental changes, which within broad age groups are remarkably similar.

Neonates. These sleep for 16 hours a day over several periods. Active sleep, an immature form of REM, is displayed, although this decreases and quiet sleep, an immature type of non-REM sleep, increases.

One-year-olds. These sleep 11 hours a day with sleep patterns increasingly like those of adults. REM sleep declines to 50% of duration, with sleep periods becoming longer and fewer.

Five-year-olds. These have 10 hours daily, with a third being REM sleep. Boys sleep longer and sleep disorders can occur.

Adolescents. These have 9 hours daily, with less REM sleep than children.

Middle age. Normal adult sleep patterns are apparent, though with increased levels of sleep disorders.

Senescence. Total sleep duration is unchanged, but REM sleep decreases to 20 % of duration, with stage 2 sleep increasing to 60 %. Sleep disturbance is common.

> **Van Cauter et al. (2000)** examined sleep studies involving males, finding that sleep decreased between 16 and 25, and 35 and 50 years of age.
>
> **Floyd et al. (2007)** reviewed nearly 400 sleep studies, finding that REM sleep decreasing by 0.6 % a decade, with its proportion increasing from age 70, although this may be due to overall sleep duration declining.
>
> **Eaton-Evans and Dugdale (1988)** found that the number of sleep periods for a baby decreases until 6 months of age and then increases until 9 months of age, then slowly decreases again, although this may be due to teething problems.

- Neonates sleeping for long periods may be an adaptive response, freeing up essential time for their parents.
- Males over 45 years old often have little stages 1–4 sleep, affecting hormone production, and this may explain why physical injuries take longer to heal.
- During senescence the decline of non-REM sleep incurs lower levels of growth hormone production, suggesting that non-REM sleep is associated with its production.

Q Outline lifespan changes in sleep.   *(9 marks)*

C Disorders of sleep

1 *Explanations for insomnia*

Insomnia takes the form of an inadequate quantity or quality of sleep, with sufferers having long-term problems initiating or maintaining sleep. About half of adults have insomnia problems, women suffering more than men, possibly because of hormonal fluctuations associated with menstruation and the menopause. Tiredness is experienced during the day, affecting physical and cognitive functioning.

Primary insomnia. One in three insomniacs are primary insomniacs, with clear underlying causes. This could be a brain abnormality affecting the neural circuits involving sleeping, or environmental stress, which can be self-perpetuating as not sleeping causes further stress, leading to a continuation of the insomnia. Other common causes are behaviour before sleep, sleep patterns and the sleeping environment: for instance, being too hot, cold or noisy.

Secondary insomnia. This is where the disorder is secondary to another medical condition.. Psychological problems, such as depression, grief and dementia, account for 50 % of cases, with physical disorders such as arthritis, diabetes and pain accounting for another 10 %.

Medicines can cause secondary insomnia, as well as alcohol, caffeine and recreational drugs. Other sleep disorders can also incur insomnia.

Duration. Insomnia can either be transient, lasting a few nights, short-term, lasting more than a few nights but less than 3 weeks, or long-term, occurring most nights and for longer than 3 weeks.

Patterns. Onset insomnia involves difficulty in getting to sleep, often associated with anxiety. Middle-of-the-night insomnia is characterised by problems in returning to sleep after waking, or waking too early. Middle insomnia involves waking in the middle of the night and/or difficulty in staying asleep, often associated with medical illnesses or physical pain. Late insomnia involves waking early in the morning, often associated with clinical depression.

Factors influencing insomnia

Apnoea. This is a medical condition where sufferers have persistent pauses in their breathing lasting for minutes and occasional loud snorts as breathing recommences. This can occur 200 times a night. Obstructive sleep apnoea is caused by blockage of the airways, often in overweight middle-aged males, while central sleep apnoea occurs due to impaired brain signals to areas associated with breathing, and happens more infrequently.

Chest (2001) found a positive correlation between insomnia and obstructive sleep apnoea, suggesting a relationship between the two

Morrell et al. (2000) found sleep apnoea more common in adults, with up to 1 in 5 sufferers, ten times the number of younger people, although the disorder tends to be more severe in the young. The difference in prevalence rates may be due to changes in the structure and function of the cardiovascular system in adults.

- Sleep apnoea can lead to insomnia being prevalent in older adults. As the population ages, there is an assumption that the disorder will grow, increasing the need for treatments.
- Doctors report increasing numbers of younger people with insomnia and sleep apnoea. This may be related to growing obesity among the young.

Personality. Research has associated personality with the onset and continuation of insomnia. Psychasthenia, a personality disorder similar to obsessive-compulsive disorder, is especially implicated. Other commonly identified factors include over-sensitivity, low self-esteem, lack of autonomy and heightened emotional arousal.

De Carvalho et al. (2003) found insomniacs to be characterised by heightened levels of anxiety and insecurity, especially among females.

Kales et al. (1976) found that 85% of insomniacs had abnormal personalities characterised by psychasthenia, elevated levels of depression and conversion hysteria. Sufferers tended to internalise psychological disturbances, producing constant emotional arousal. This suggests that a psychophysiological mechanism underpins insomnia.

- Rather than personality traits leading to insomnia, it may be that insomnia creates changes in personality.
- Research indicates that treating abnormal personality traits and disorders is more successful in reducing insomnia than treating insomnia to try and address personality defects, implying that abnormal personality traits are the causal factor.

Furukawa (2009) found that behavioural treatments can address personality-linked insomnia, suggesting that malaptive learning experiences are important factors.

Q (a) Outline two forms of insomnia. *(5 marks)*
(b) Outline and evaluate explanations for insomnia. *(20 marks)*

2 *Explanations for other sleep disorders*

Sleep walking. *Somnambulism* refers to activities occurring unconsciously when asleep that normally occur when awake: for example, eating, cleaning and walking, and even sending nonsensical e-mails, having sex and committing murder. It is more prevalent in childhood, declining sharply in adulthood. Somnambulism tends to be associated with personality disorders, especially ones relating to anxiety.

Incidents of somnambulism occur during NREM with the sufferer's eyes open, seemingly awake. However, speech tends to be gibberish and the episode is not recalled. The disorder places the sufferer at risk of injury or abuse.

Hublin et al. (1997) found somnambulism more common among children, with 20% affected. In adults the rate is only 2%, indicating that the condition is linked to development and maturation.

Nowak (2004) reported on an Australian woman who left her house to have somnambulistic sex with strangers. She had had a history of sleep walking and talking since childhood.

Broughton (1968) found somnambulism to be heritable, with sufferers ten times more likely than the general population to have close relatives with the disorder, suggesting a genetic factor.

Kales and Kales (1975) found that somnambulistic episodes generally occur in stage 3 and 4 sleep.

- Somnambulism has been used as a defence against murder charges. Kenneth Parks was acquitted in 1987 of killing his in-laws in Canada due to non-insane automatism.
- Somnambulism has been alleviated by avoiding risk factors, such as excitatory activities, using techniques such as meditation before sleeping and sleeping in a safe environment.
- Children may have higher incidences of somnambulism because they spend long amounts of time in slow wave sleep, where the condition tends to occur. Children are also observed more while asleep, therefore episodes are more likely to be detected.
- The current focus of research is that a group of sleep disorders known as parasomnias, such as somnambulism, sleep terrors, etc. share a common genetic cause.

Narcolepsy. This is a sleep disorder characterised by disruption to the sleep–wake cycle with sufferers falling asleep at unexpected times, often in mid-activity. Sufferers feel sleepy during the day, appearing drunk. Microsleeps are common, from which the sufferer awakes without realising they have been asleep.

Another symptom is *cataplexy*, where muscular control is lost, usually as a result of being excited.

Sleep paralysis can occur when the brain awakes from an REM state, leaving the body paralysed, with the sufferer fully conscious. Terrifying hallucinations and a sense of danger can also occur.

Narcolepsy is often perceived as a dream, with dream-like objects appearing alongside objects in vision. The condition usually appears in adolescence and is believed to originate from a genetic abnormality. Other factors may be a shortage of the neurotransmitter hypocretin, or an autoimmune disease.

Montplaisir (2007) found that sufferers had a higher percentage of REM sleep, although this may be a cause or effect of the condition.

Mignot et al. (1999) found a defective gene, hypocretin receptor 2, in dogs, one of the few species suffering from narcolepsy. The defective form of the gene inhibits wakefulness, suggesting a genetic basis to the disorder.

Hufford (1982) reports on an ancient sleep paralysis myth, hag riding. This explains people's belief in witches, but also suggests that narcolepsy is long lasting, implying it to be hereditary. This is backed up by such legends being cross-cultural; **Kanashibari (1993)** reports similar myths in Japan.

- It is hoped that research into narcolepsy may produce sleeping drugs more closely mimicking natural brain chemistry.
- The bizarre hallucinations that sufferers experience are suggested by Blackmore and Cox (2008) as explaining the experience of alien abduction that people sometimes report undergoing.
- Using samples based on patient associations can create bias, as only certain types of sufferers may join the association.
- The identification of genes associated with the disorder does not mean that there is a definite genetic cause. Researchers stress the need to identify environmental triggers.

Q Discuss explanations for two sleep disorders.   *(25 marks)*

A Theories of perceptual organisation

1 Gregory's top-down/indirect theory

Perception is seen as actively searching for the best interpretation of sensory data based on previous experience and therefore involves going beyond the immediate data. We learn to perceive by interacting with our world. Perception is an unconscious process, occurring indirectly, as it involves higher level (top-down) processing. Gregory believes that much sensory data is impoverished, incomplete or ambiguous, and therefore we need to go beyond it, making inferences in order to perceive. Sometimes this can lead to errors (e.g. visual illusions).

The idea of *perceptual set* is important, being a readiness to perceive certain features of sensory data based on previous experience, motivational and emotional factors, and cultural influences.

Expectation. This is a feature of Gregory's theory where we perceive what we expect to see based on previous experience.

> **Aarts and Dijksterhuis (2002)** influenced estimates of a man's walking speed by creating an expectation of what it should be, by first asking participants to think about fast or slow animals. This shows how experience can bias perception, demonstrating that it is both an indirect and active process, supporting the idea of perceptual set.

> **Leeper (1935)** showed participants an ambiguous picture, which could be seen as a young or an old woman. Participants initially given a description or picture of a young woman saw a young woman and those described or shown an old woman saw an old woman, indicating that expectation based on previous experience can determine perception in an indirect fashion.

Motivational and emotional factors. These affect perception by creating a bias to perceive, or not, certain features of incoming sensory data. *Perceptual defence* is an important concept, where emotionally threatening stimuli take longer to perceive.

> **Lazarus and McCleary (1951)** found that nonsense syllables which were presented so fast that they could not be consciously perceived, raised anxiety levels if previously paired with electric shocks, supporting the idea of emotional factors unconsciously influencing perception.

> **Solley and Haigh (1948)** found that children drew a bigger Santa and sack of toys as Christmas approached, but that after it had passed Santa and his sack shrunk, indicating that motivational factors influence perception.

> **McGinnies (1949)** found that emotionally threatening words took longer to recognise than neutral ones, supporting the idea of perceptual defence and emotional factors influencing perception. However, the results may be due to the embarrassment of speaking the words aloud. **Bitterman and Kniffin (1953)** found no differences in recognition time if the words were written down.

Cultural influences. These affect perceptual set by predisposing people to perceive features of an environment in a certain way. Therefore people from different cultural backgrounds sometimes perceive identical sensory information differently.

Pettigrew et al. (1978) presented a picture of one South African ethnic group to one eye of a participant and another ethnic group to the other eye. White South Africans could not distinguish between black and mixed-race people, suggesting that the cultural influence of their racial prejudice affected perception.

Segall (1963) found that Africans living in open country, where occasional vertical objects were important features, were susceptible to the horizontal–vertical illusion, while those living in dense jungle were unlikely to see the illusion, implying that physical environment shapes cultural influences, which affects perception.

Evaluation of Gregory's theory

- Gregory predicts that, once we understand why we experience an illusion, our perception is modified and we will not experience it any more. But we do, casting doubt on Gregory's explanation.
- The theory has aided understanding of perception and has stimulated interest and research in the subject area.
- Gregory possibly underestimates the richness of sensory data and that it may be possible to perceive directly from it. This misbelief could have arisen because laboratory experiments present incomplete or isolated stimuli, while in the real world sensory data are more informative and complete.
- There is a logical sense to the theory that we make inferences based on previous experience when viewing conditions that are incomplete or ambiguous.

Q Describe and evaluate Gregory's top-down/indirect theory of perception.   *(25 marks)*

2 | *Gibson's direct/bottom up theory*

Gibson believes that the *optic array* (the pattern of light hitting our eyes) is a rich enough source of sensory data to permit direct perception. Our movements and those of objects within an environment assist this process. This involves innate mechanisms and therefore we do not need to learn from experience. Gibson sees perception occurring due to direct perception of invariants, constant features of the optical array containing enough sensory information to allow direct perception (e.g. spatial arrangements). No inferences from previous experience are necessary or any higher information processing. It is a bottom-up process, as perception is constructed directly from sensory information.

The optic array. This is composed of patterned light hitting our eyes. It is ever-changing due to the movements of ourselves and objects within the physical environment. The optical array contains invariant (constant) sources of information. There are several types, all of which contribute to allow direct perception from the sensory information.

Optic flow patterns. These are unambiguous sources of information concerning height, distance and speed that directly inform perception. As we move around, distant objects appear to move slowly, while closer objects seem to move more quickly. This depth cue is known as *motion parallax*.

Johansson (1973) found that a black-clad actor wearing lights on his joints, walking in a darkened room, was perceivable as a moving person, demonstrating the importance of movement in determining optic flow patterns.

Maher and West (1993) filmed moving black-clad animals with lights on their joints, finding that the species of animal was recognisable. This demonstrates the strength of movement information in determining optic flow patterns and shows that there is enough sensory information for perception to occur directly

Texture gradient. This is surface patterns providing sensory information about the depth, shape, etc. of objects. Physical objects possess surfaces with different textures, allowing direct perception of distance, depth and spatial awareness. Due to movements, the 'flow' of texture gradients provides rich sources of sensory information. Motion parallax and *linear perspective*, a depth cue provided by lines seemingly converging as they become distant, permit direct availability to the senses of the third dimension of depth.

Gibson and Bridgeman (1987) found that participants could identify objects and their colour, and say whether they were lying flat etc. from photographs of surface textures, suggesting that there is sufficient sensory information in surface textures to permit direct perception.

Frichtel et al. (2006) found that 4-month-old infants could perceive from texture gradients, implying the ability to be innate.

Horizon ratios. These concern the position of objects in relation to the horizon. Objects of different sizes at equal distances from an observer have different horizon ratios. Therefore, horizon ratios provide another source of invariant sensory information allowing direct perception.

Creem-Regehr et al. (2003) found restricting viewing conditions did not affect the ability to judge distances using horizon-ratio information, suggesting this form of invariant sensory information is a powerful means of establishing direct perception .

Affordances. These involve attaching meaning to sensory information. They concern the quality of objects to permit actions to be carried out upon them (action possibilities): for example, a brush 'affords' sweeping the floor. Gibson saw affordances as being directly perceivable, thus rejecting Gregory's belief that the meaning of objects is stored in long-term memory from experience.

Warren (1984) studied whether participants could judge if staircases portrayed with differently proportioned steps could 'afford' to be climbed. This was dependent on the length of a participant's leg. Participants proved to be sensitive to the affordance of 'climbability', seemingly from the invariant properties of the light reflected from the staircases, providing some support for the concept of affordances not being reliant on experience.

▶ ## Evaluation of Gibson's theory

- Gibson's theory explains how perception occurs so quickly, which Gregory's theory cannot do.
- Gibson's theory has led to greater understanding, interest and research into perception. For instance, Gaver (1996) applied the idea of affordances into designing computer displays.
- A practical application of Gibson's theory is putting parallel lines increasingly close together as a road junction nears, giving a false impression of speed to slow drivers down.
- The idea that the optical array provides direct information about what objects allow us to do (affordances) seems unlikely. Knowledge about objects is affected by cultural influences, experience and emotions.

Q Compare Gregory's top-down (indirect) and Gibson's bottom-up (direct) theories of perception.

(25 marks)

B Development of perception

1 ## *The development of perceptual abilities*

Perception is made up of several abilities, some more learned in nature, others more innate. A baby has some basic perceptual abilities, incurring immediate survival value, which allow it to interact with the environment. Thus perceptual abilities become shaped to suit an individual's needs and environment, and therefore complex abilities tend to be affected more by learning.

Perceptual abilities

Depth/distance. This involves perceiving the environment as three-dimensional and judging distances of objects from each other and ourselves. Cues can be *monocular* (apparent to one eye) and *binocular* (apparent to both eyes), and these are divisible into *primary* (not dependent on learning) and *secondary* (dependent on learning). Infants use primary cues, as they are innate and therefore appear first.

Visual constancies. These concern how objects appear to remain constant and unchanging regardless of the viewing conditions. This has a survival value, as an ordered, predictable world is a safer place to interact with.

Neonate studies

Perceptual abilities present at birth are assumed to be innate, as learning experiences have not occurred. Neonate studies present ethical and practical challenges, and various methodologies have been developed, such as preference studies (which stimuli is preferred), sucking, heart/breathing rate (indicating interest), reinforcement (showing recognition) and brain scans (showing neural activity).

Depth/distance research

Gibson and Walk (1960) found that babies would not cross an apparent vertical drop, suggesting that depth perception is innate.

Bower et al. (1970) found that neonates shielded their eyes at approaching objects, also suggesting that depth perception is innate.

Slater et al. (1984) found that neonates prefer to look at a three-dimensional stimulus rather than a photograph of it, suggesting that depth perception is innate or develops soon after birth.

Visual constancies research

Shape

Imura et al. (2008) found that sensitivity to shading and line junctions as a means of determining shape constancy appears between 6 and 7 months of age.

Size

Bower (1966) trained infants to respond to a certain cube at a certain distance. Other cubes of differing sizes and at various distances were presented and infants mainly responded to the cube of the same size, regardless of retinal image, suggesting that size constancy occurs early in life.

Colour

Dannemiller and Hanko (1987) found that infants could recognise familiar colours under some conditions, but not all, indicating that some colour constancy appears early in life, but needs time to develop.

- A neonate's visual system is not well developed at birth, making it problematic to find what skills are innate.
- Neonates lose concentration easily, making research short term and results possibly invalid.

- Neonate studies involve making inferences about their perceptual world. However, these may not be accurate and could be prone to researcher bias.
- Innate abilities may not be apparent at birth, but emerge later as a result of biological maturation without any learning required.

Cross-cultural studies

If people from different cultures have similar perceptual abilities, it is assumed that those abilities are innate. Conversely, if abilities are different, it is assumed they are learned.

Allport and Pettigrew (1957) found that people of Western cultures perceive the rotating trapezoid illusion, interpreting it as a window. Rural Zulus, with no experience of windows, do not perceive the illusion, supporting the idea that perceptual abilities are learned.

Turnbull (1961) reported a forest pygmy with no experience of long-distance cues, who, when taken to savannah grassland, thought distant buffalo were insects, suggesting that depth cues necessary for size constancy are learned.

Montello (2006) performed a meta-analysis of cross-cultural studies of depth/distance, finding cultural differences to be fairly small. This suggests that these perceptual abilities are innate.

- Cross-cultural research has focused mainly on visual illusions, which may not relate to more everyday perceptual abilities.
- The use of depth cues in pictures as a research tool has been criticised, as they do not relate to the actual world.
- Cross-cultural studies are susceptible to biased interpretation, especially in terms of the culture of the researcher.
- It is difficult with cross-cultural studies to obtain similar samples and replicate methodologies exactly, decreasing the validity of findings.

Q Outline the development of perceptual abilities. *(9 marks)*

2 *The nature/nurture debate*

The debate concerns whether human qualities are innate (genetic) or learned (environmental), and development of abilities is seen as occurring due either to biological maturation (nature) or to experience (nurture). Some perceptual abilities seem more innate, while others seem more learned.

Interactionism views perceptual skills as a combination of innate and learned factors. Basic skills are innate and useful for immediate survival, while complex skills are learned and modifiable to suit different and changing environments.

Gibson favours nature, as environmental experiences are not seen as necessary to perceive, while Gregory favours nurture, believing there is a role for environmental experiences.

Animal studies. These often use sensory deprivation to determine what (if any) sensory experiences are necessary for perceptual development.

Hubel and Weisel (1982) found that cats' innate perceptual skills need environmental experience to develop fully, showing how nature and nurture interact to form perceptual abilities.

Hubel and Weisel (1962) found that cats have specialist neurons in their visual cortex for specific perceptual tasks, suggesting that pattern recognition has a biological basis, and therefore supporting the nurture viewpoint.

Reisen (1965) found that the environmental experience of seeing patterned light is required to develop complex perceptual skills in chimps. This supports nature.

- There are problems generalising from animals to humans. Human perception consists of complex skills, needing environmental input to develop fully. Human perception is more modifiable too; animals often cannot adjust to new perceptual realities, while humans sometimes can.
- Physical and psychological harm caused by animal experiments raises ethical concerns. Cost–benefit analysis can be used as justification: for example, if research leads to treatments for visual impairments.

Perceptual readjustment studies. These attempt to see if it is possible to adapt to different perceptual worlds. If it is, then it is taken as evidence to support nurture.

Sperry (1943) rotated salamanders' eyes, finding that they could not adjust to their new perceptual world. This favours the nature side of the debate.

Snyder and Pronko (1852) put inversing–reversing goggles on participants, finding they could adjust to an upside-down, back-to-front world. This suggests that the ability was learned, thus supporting nature.

- Studies show that humans can readjust. However, they may actually have learned to adapt their motor responses rather than adapt their perceptual abilities, casting doubt on the nature side of the debate
- Research shows that humans can make perceptual readjustments. As an innate system would not permit this, it suggests that learning plays a major role in the development of perception, supporting nature.

Cataract studies. When people have cataracts removed from their eyes, whatever perceptual abilities they exhibit are assumed to be innate.

Gregory and Wallace (1963) reported on a man with cataracts from birth, removed at age 52. He could visually recognise objects known from touch, but could not learn to recognise new objects by vision alone or learn to judge distances, supporting the nature viewpoint.

Von Senden (1960) reviewed 65 cataract removal cases, finding that they generally did not adjust to new perceptual worlds, again supporting the nature argument.

- Cataract case studies are rare and may not be representative. Most patients have had visual experiences from before they developed cataracts, and therefore perceptual abilities, evident when cataracts are removed, may not be innate.
- Physical damage to the visual system may have occurred during the time of blindness and this may be responsible for lack of perceptual abilities, casting doubts on the validity of conclusions drawn from cataract removal studies.

Conclusions

The nature/nurture debate is difficult to resolve. Different research methods can produce conflicting results, possibly because perception should be researched not as a whole ability, but as a series of interrelated individual abilities, with each one being studied separately. Different research methodologies have their drawbacks too, such as generalising from animal studies, or ascertaining what neonates can see. The best conclusion is probably one considering inputs from both nature and nurture.

Q Discuss the nature/nurture debate in relation to perceptual development.   *(25 marks)*

C Face recognition and visual agnosias

Face recognition is the process by which human faces are interpreted and understood. Humans seem innately attracted to faces, and this incurs a survival value as it helps create attachments and allows recognition of people, which is important for social interactions.

1 Bruce and Young's theory of face recognition

This is a stage theory, with face recognition involving two different mechanisms:

Familiar faces — structural encoding followed by face recognition nodes, person identity nodes and name generation.

Unfamiliar faces — structural encoding followed by expression analysis, facial speech analysis and directed visual processing.

To become familiar, a face must be seen several times so that a firm representation is stored. Therefore the structural encoding, based on a pictorial code, improves.

Face recognition is a holistic process, where facial features, involving eight independent sub-processes working together, are processed collectively. Different processing modules process different types of information, such as facial expression.

Sub-components of face recognition

Type of component	Description of component
Structural encoding	Creation of descriptions and representations of faces
Expression analysis	Analysis of facial characteristics to infer emotional state
Facial speech analysis	Analysis of facial movements to comprehend speech
Directed visual processing	Selective processing of specific facial data
Facial recognition nodes	Stored structural descriptions of familiar faces
Person identity nodes	Stored information about familiar people
Name generation	Separate store for names
Cognitive storage	Extra information that aids the recognition process

The theory states that two types of information are held on people:

Visually derived semantic code — details related to physical aspects, such as gender or race.

Identity-specific semantic code — biographical details not related to physical aspects, such as hobbies and achievements.

Retrieval of information from the identity-specific semantic code permits recognition of faces.

The theory proposes two types of node:

Face recognition node (FRN) — containing structural information on faces.

Person identity node (PIN) — containing identity-specific information.

The theory explains how facial information is analysed. Recognition of familiar faces is seen to involve matching results of structural encoding and stored structural codes that describe familiar faces, located in the FRNs; then identity-specific semantic codes are obtained from the PINs so that name codes can be retrieved. Both facial features and the configuration of features are used to recognise faces as being familiar.

Bruce and Valentine (1988) found that expressive movements, such as smiling, convey little variant information to aid identification, suggesting that invariant information is used more to perform face recognition.

Ellis et al. (1979) found that external facial features, such as hairstyles, are used to recognise unknown faces, while internal features, such as noses, are used with familiar faces. Only static pictures of faces were used, so the results may not reflect how face recognition occurs in real life.

Sergent (1984) presented two identikit faces that differed on one or two facial features, such as shape of eyes or chin. Deciding if faces were different occurred faster when they varied on two features, implying that facial features are processed collectively (configural processing) rather than independently.

Malone et al. (1982) reported on a man able to recognise familiar faces, but not able to match up photos of unknown faces; and a man unable to recognise known faces, but who could match up photos of unknown people. This suggests damage to different brain areas, implying that familiar and unfamiliar faces are processed differently and therefore supporting Bruce and Young's model.

- One aspect not fully understood is the relationship between face recognition and object recognition, although case studies of visual agnosia have shed light on this area.
- The theory is backed up by case studies of visual agnosias indicating that face recognition consists of independent sub-components.
- The theory's central idea, that face recognition is a holistic process consisting of a series of independent stages, is generally accepted, lending support to the theory.
- The theory sees the processing of facial information as occurring in sequential fashion. This is supported by evidence.
- The theory has led to the development of practical applications, such as computer security systems that use face recognition software.
- The theory is not without criticism. It cannot explain how unfamiliar face recognition occurs or how familiarity is achieved, weakening support for the theory.
- Many parts of the theory are well explained and have empirical support. But it is not clear how some sub-components, such as cognitive storage, work in helping to determine face recognition.

Q Outline and evaluate Bruce and Young's theory of face recognition. *(25 marks)*

2 Case studies of prosopagnosia

Sufferers of visual agnosias, of which prosopagnosia is a type, do not have damage to their visual systems, but cannot use or make sense of certain visual information. Visual agnosias often result from stroke damage to the posterior occipital and/or the temporal lobes of the brain. Sufferers can usually describe objects or faces in terms of features and colours etc., but cannot name them even if familiar.

It was believed that the perception of objects and faces involved processing by the same neural mechanisms. However, case studies have indicated that there might be a specific processor for faces.

Prosopagnosia is associated specifically with damage to the fusiform gyrus brain area and sufferers can generally recognise objects, but not faces. There are different types and levels of prosopagnosia, indicating that each stage of face recognition can be affected, and giving strength to Bruce and Young's notion that face recognition consists of sequential stages. There is no long-term effective treatment for the condition, but a fuller understanding may lead to one.

Dailey and Cottrell (1999) provided an explanation of how a separate face-processing mechanism could evolve, based on the idea of the visual system developing a processing sub-system useful for the recognition of faces, occurring as a natural response to a child's developmental environment: for instance, a child's need to identify faces from an early age.

Bauer (1984) found a patient whose galvanic skin response went up when looking at a familiar face and the correct name was read out, suggesting that although face recognition may not appear present at a conscious level, unconsciously it is there.

Brunsdon et al. (2006) reported on a boy who could not recognise familiar or unfamiliar faces, suggesting that his damage was at the level of structural encoding, right at the beginning of the face recognition process.

Kurucz et al. (1979) reported on prosopagnosics who could name familiar faces, but could not identify their facial expression, while **Bruyer et al. (1983)** had a patient unable to name familiar faces, but who could understand their facial expressions, suggesting that facial expression analysis and name generation are separate components of face recognition.

Campbell et al. (1986) found a prosopagnosic who was unable to name familiar faces, or identify their facial expressions, but who could perform speech analysis, suggesting that facial speech analysis, in line with the theory, is a separate component of face recognition.

Kanwisher et al. (1997) found fMRI scans suggested that face recognition involves a separate processing mechanism with the fusiform gyrus more active in face recognition than in object recognition, implying that this brain area is associated specifically with face recognition processing.

- Humphreys and Riddoch (1987) cast doubt on the idea of object and face recognition being processed separately by different mechanisms. They suggest that face recognition may simply be a more complex form of object recognition. If so, slight damage to a general-purpose recognition system would affect object recognition less than face recognition. Supporting this is the fact that prosopagnosics tend to have slight damage to object recognition and severe damage to face recognition.
- Doubts are also cast by Gauthier et al. (2000) on the idea of separate processing mechanisms. Faces may just be complex objects taking more skill to recognise. This is supported by the fusiform gyrus being activated not only during face recognition, but in object discrimination too, implying that the fusiform gyrus cannot be specifically involved in face recognition.
- Evidence generally shows that prosopagnosia affects face recognition in different ways, suggesting that face recognition does occur as a holistic process of sequential, independent sub-components.
- There is a concern as to how representative case studies are of the general population, especially as they involve people with abnormal brain conditions.

Q Evaluate explanations of prosopagnosia. *(16 marks)*

3 Relationships

A The formation, maintenance and breakdown of romantic relationships

1 Theories of the formation, maintenance and breakdown of romantic relationships

Formation

The sociobiological explanation. This is an evolutionary theory with differing focus between genders. Males are never certain of paternity and produce lots of sperm, therefore their best strategy is to have multiple partners. Males value signs of fertility, such as smooth skin and faithfulness, not wanting to waste resources raising someone else's child. Females produce few eggs, but are certain of maternity and seek genetically strong children by being selective in choosing partners and getting them to invest resources. Females look for kindness, indicating a willingness to share resources.

> **Dunbar (1995)** analysed personal advertisements, finding that males sought youthfulness and attractiveness more than females. This supports the sociobiological idea that males and females have different reasons for forming relationships.
>
> **Davis (1990)** analysed personal advertisements, finding that men look for health and attractiveness, while offering resources. Females look for resources and status, while offering beauty and youth, supporting the evolutionary theory of gender differences in relationship formation.

- The theory presumes heterosexuality, that children are wanted and that all relationships are sexual; it is therefore oversimplified.
- The explanation is reductionist, seeing relationships purely as a means of reproduction.
- The explanation supports gender stereotypes of housebound women and sexually promiscuous males.
- The theory offers a plausible explanation for the evolution of mate preferences.

Reinforcement and need satisfaction. This theory sees conditioning as an explanation for relationship formation. A person may reward us directly by meeting psychological needs for love and sex, or indirectly because they are associated with pleasant circumstances, therefore we are more likely to form a relationship. If we associate a person with being in a good mood, or removing a negative mood, we find them attractive, increasing the chances of relationship formation.

> **Cunningham (1988)** studied males who watched a happy or sad film, then interacted with a female. More positive interactions came from those watching the happy film, supporting the explanation.
>
> **May and Hamilton (1980)** asked females to rate photos of males, while nice or unpleasant music was played. Those with nice music rated the males as more attractive, supporting the theory.

- Many non-Western cultures feature relationships without regard for receiving rewards or prioritising selfish needs. Therefore the theory cannot account for cultural differences.
- The explanation does not account for gender differences. Women focus more on the needs of others and males and females find different things rewarding, suggesting that the explanation is oversimplified.

Maintenance

Social exchange theory. This explains relationships in terms of maximising benefits and minimising costs. There is a mutual exchange of rewards between partners, such as friendship, and the costs of being in the relationship, such as freedoms given up. Rewards are assessed by comparisons:

- *The comparison level* (CL). Rewards are compared to costs in order to judge profits.
- *The comparison level for alternative relationships* (Clalt). Rewards and costs are compared against perceived rewards and costs for possible alternative relationships.

Relationships are maintained if rewards exceed costs, and if profit levels are not exceeded by possible alternative relationships.

Rusbult (1983) found that costs and rewards of relationships were compared to costs and rewards of potential alternative relationships to decide if relationships should be maintained, supporting the theory.

Hatfield (1979) looked at people who felt over or under-benefited. The under-benefited felt angry and deprived, while the over-benefited felt guilty and uncomfortable, supporting the theory by suggesting that, regardless of whether individuals are benefited, they may not desire to maintain a relationship.

- Argyle (1988) criticised methodologies used to evaluate social exchange theory, declaring them contrived and artificial with little relevance to real life.
- Research has tended to concentrate on short-term consequences of relationships rather than more important long-term maintenance.
- The theory applies to people who 'keep score'. Murstein et al. (1977) devised the exchange orientation tool to identify such scorekeepers, who are suspicious and insecure, suggesting that the theory suits relationships lacking confidence and mutual trust.

Equity theory. This perceives individuals as motivated to achieve fairness and to feel dissatisfied with inequity (unfairness). Maintenance occurs through balance and stability. Relationships where individuals put in more than they receive, or receive more than they put in, are inequitable, leading to dissatisfaction and possible dissolution.

Relationships may alternate between periods of perceived balance and imbalance, with individuals being motivated to return to equity. The greater the perceived imbalance, the greater the efforts to realign relationships, if viable.

Yum et al. (2009) looked at various types of heterosexual romantic relationships in different cultures. As predicted by equity theory, maintenance strategies differed, suggesting that equity theory can be applied cross-culturally.

Canary and Stafford (1992) assessed the degree of equity in romantic relationships, finding a link between the degree of perceived equity and the prevalence of maintenance strategies, implying that equitable theories are maintained.

- Equity may be more important to females. Hoschchild and Machung (1989) found that women do most work in making relationships equitable, suggesting that the theory is gender biased.
- Mills and Clark (1982) believe that it is not possible to assess equity in loving relationships, as much input is emotional and unquantifiable and to do so diminishes the quality of love.

Breakdown

Duck's stage theory. Duck (1984) proposed a stage theory of dissolution.

Phase of dissolution	Description
Intra-psychic phase	One partner privately perceives dissatisfaction with the relationship.
Dyadic phase	The dissatisfaction is discussed. If not resolved, there is a move to the next stage.
Social phase	The breakdown is made public. Negotiation about children, finances, etc, with wider families and friends becoming involved.
Grave-dressing phase	Establish post-relationship view of the break-up, protecting self-esteem and rebuilding life towards new relationship.

Kassin (1996) found women more likely to stress unhappiness and incompatibility as reasons for dissolution, while men blame lack of sex. Women wish to remain friends, while males want clean breaks, implying that the model does not consider gender differences.

Akert (1992) found that instigators of break-ups suffer less negative consequences than non-instigators, suggesting that the model does not explain individual differences in the effects of dissolution.

- The model does not explain cultural differences in relationship dissolution. Many non-Western cultures have arranged marriages, which can be more permanent and involve whole families in crises.
- The model has practical applications in counselling. Assessing which phase a couple are in helps in forming strategies to rescue relationships.
- The model is plausible, relating to many people's experiences of relationship dissolution.

Lee's five-stage model. Lee (1984) proposed a five-stage model of relationship dissolution, seeing dissolution as a process occurring over time, rather than as a single event.

Stage of dissolution	Description
Dissatisfaction	An individual becomes dissatisfied with the relationship.
Exposure	Dissatisfaction is revealed to one's partner.
Negotiation	Discussion occurs over the nature of the dissatisfaction.
Resolution	Attempts are made to resolve the dissatisfaction.
Termination	If the dissatisfaction is not resolved, the relationship ends.

Lee (1984) surveyed non-marital romantic relationship breakdowns, finding that negotiation and exposure were most distressing and emotionally exhausting. Individuals who missed out stages, going straight to termination, had less intimate relationships. Those going through stages in lengthy and exhaustive fashion, felt attracted to former partners after termination and felt lost and lonely.

Argyle and Henderson (1984) found that rule violations caused breakdowns, with jealousy, lack of tolerance for third-party relationships, disclosing confidences, not volunteering help and public criticism most critical.

- Lee's theory is reductionist, focusing only on romantic, heterosexual relationships, suggesting that it is not applicable to friendships, homosexual relationships, etc.
- Lee's theory is more positive than Duck's, seeing more opportunities for problematic relationships to be saved.
- Stage theories describe the process of dissolution, but do not provide explanations of why the process occurs.
- Lee only studied students in pre-marital relationships, which may not relate to long-term relationships.

Q **(a)** Outline two theories of the maintenance of romantic relationships.   *(9 marks)*
   (b) Evaluate one of the theories outlined in part (a).   *16 marks)*

B Human reproductive behaviour

1 Relationship between sexual selection and reproductive behaviour

Sexual selection concerns the selection of characteristics increasing reproductive success, namely producing healthy children who survive to sexual maturity.

There are differences between male and female sexual behaviour, as they are subject to different selective pressures.

Males produce lots of small, highly mobile sperm and can fertilise many females at little cost to reproductive potential. They are not sure of paternity and so natural selection favours male behaviours maximising the number of potential pregnancies, resulting in intrasexual competition between males and polygamy, where one individual mates with many partners. Males seek signs of fertility, such as childbearing hips.

For females, each egg represents a sizeable reproductive investment, although she is always sure of maternity. Natural selection favours female behaviours maximising chances of potential reproductions being successful, such as careful mate selection, monogamy and high parental investment. Females seek signs of genetic fitness, such as resource richness, and indulge in intersexual competition, choosing males from those available.

Singh (1993) found that males prefer females with a waist ratio of 0.7:1, suggesting choice on the basis of potential fertility.

Penton-Voak et al. (2001) found that females prefer males with greater facial symmetry, an indication of developmental stability that would be passed on to her sons, increasing reproductive potential.

Clark and Hatfield (1989) found that males are more promiscuous, supporting the idea of gender-based differences in sexual selection.

Buss (1989) tested participants from 37 cultures, finding that males prefer young, physically attractive females, while females prefer resource-rich, ambitious, industrious males, supporting the gender-based predictions of sexual selection in humans.

Boone (1986) found that females prefer older males with resources, while **Kenrick and Keefe (1992)** found that males prefer younger females, supporting the theory.

Male strategies

Courtship rituals. These allow males to compete and display genetic potential. Miller (1997) believes that evolution shaped cultural aspects, such as humour to attract sexual partners.

Size. Males evolved to be bigger, demonstrating strength for success against other males.

Sperm competition. Natural selection acted upon males, making them more competitive by producing larger testicles, more copious ejaculations and faster-swimming sperm.

Jealousy. Males fear spending resources raising another male's child. Buss (1993) found that men feared partners being sexually unfaithful, while females feared emotional unfaithfulness, demonstrating the male fear of cuckoldry and the female fear of partners spending resources on other females.

Sneak copulation. Males will mate with other females if given the opportunity. Women gain, as having different fathers brings wider genetic diversity to their children, increasing survival chances.

Males of polygamous species are under great selective pressure to exhibit sexual display characteristics. **Kirkpatrick (1987)** found that this created a runaway process, resulting in features maladaptive in circumstances other than courtship. This supports the handicap hypothesis.

Birkhead (1990) found that 8% of Zebra finch offspring came from females' sneaky copulations with non-partner males, supporting the idea of sneak copulations.

There is evidence from the animal kingdom supporting the idea of sperm competition. **Dewsbury (1984)** reported that rats have a mating system where multiple males mate with females, especially at high population densities. Rats have large testicles, producing copious sperm and increasing reproduction chances.

- It is difficult to identify and separate effects of sexual selection from natural selection, making research problematic.
- Evolutionary theory is often retrospective and therefore difficult to test.

Female strategies

The sexy sons hypothesis. Females select attractive males who will produce sons with similar attractive features, increasing reproductive fitness.

Attractive characteristics have an adaptive advantage and natural selection favours their enhancement, until they 'run away', becoming bizarre, such as the highly decorated bowers that male Bowerbirds construct to attract females.

Handicap hypothesis. Zahavi (1975) believes that females select males with handicaps because it advertises their ability to thrive despite handicaps, demonstrating superior genetic quality.

This may be why females find males who can drink alcohol or take drugs in large amounts attractive, as they are demonstrating their ability to handle toxins, a sign of genetic fitness.

Partridge (1980) allowed female fruit flies to mate freely or have forced random matings. Offspring of free-choice matings had greater competitive ability, suggesting that females improve reproductive success by selection of partners.

Moller (1992) reported that females choose males with symmetrical features, as only good genetic quality males produce them, supporting the handicap hypothesis.

- Female choosiness and male promiscuity can be explained by gender role socialisation.
- Care should be taken when generalising the findings of animal studies on to humans.

Q Discuss the relationship between sexual selection and human reproductive behaviour.
(25 marks)

2 *Evolutionary explanations of parental investment*

Parental investment increases children's survival chances at the expense of parents' ability to invest in other children. Gender differences in male and female sexual strategies, due to different selective pressures, have led to gender differences in parental investment.

Paternal certainty. With internal fertilisation, males are more likely to desert than with external fertilisation, as they are unsure of paternity.

Order of gamete release. Internal fertilisation gives males the chance to desert and leave childcare duties to the female, while with external fertilisation the situation is reversed.

Monogamy. In species with offspring born at early stages of development, or with intensive childcare, pair bonds are exclusive and enduring, increasing offsprings' survival chances.

Parental certainty. Maternal grandparents know that grandchildren are genetically related. Therefore, more care and resource allocation comes from maternal grandparents than paternal ones.

Pollett et al. (2007) found that maternal grandparents had more contact with grandchildren than paternal grandparents, fitting predictions of parental certainty.

Daly (1979) reports that, in some mammals and birds, monogamy and bi-parental care is apparent because the males contribute to care of the young, supporting predictions for monogamy.

Gross and Shine (1981) report that with internal fertilisation, parental care is carried out by females in 86% of species; while with external fertilisation, parental care is carried out by males in 70% of species, supporting predictions based on paternal certainty.

- Dawkins and Carlisle (1976) found that in 36 out of 46 species with simultaneous gamete release, where both sexes have equal chances of deserting, males provide the monoparental care, refuting the prediction.
- Krebs and Davies (1981) report that it is not always true that external fertilisation leads to increased paternal certainty. In Sunfishes, cuckoldry occurs during the female's egg positioning.
- Andersson et al. (1999) looked at investments by fathers in the education of biological and stepchildren, finding that they are highest when fathers live with the biological mother of their children, but that otherwise investments were equal, weakening evolutionary theory. Maybe men invest in stepchildren to demonstrate their resource richness, increasing their attractiveness to females.

Parent–offspring conflict

Children influence parental investment. Parents have equal investments in offspring, but the resources allocated decrease as more are born and as children age. However, children try to get parents to invest more at the expense of other offspring, creating sibling rivalry.

Parent–offspring rivalry occurs before birth when mothers experience high-blood pressure due to foetuses secreting hormones to gain more nutrition.

Children use various strategies to manipulate parents into allocating them resources, such as crying and smiling. These occur as solitary acts, or ones performed at the expense of siblings' needs.

Older parents tolerate young infants' demands more, because if they are not having more children, they can centre resources on existing ones.

Sulloway (2001) found spotted hyenas' sibling rivalries occur when subsequent cubs are born, with 25% of cubs killed by siblings

Haig (1993) found women experiencing high-blood pressure have fewer spontaneous abortions, while Xiong et al. (2000) found they have larger babies, suggesting high blood pressure has an adaptive advantage in producing healthier babies

Rimm (2002) found intense sibling rivalry when children are close in age and need resource investment more. Sibling rivalry was also intense when one sibling was gifted, presumably as an attempt to stop the talented sibling receiving advantageous proportions of parental resources.

- A child's temper tantrums can be seen in an evolutionary light as an attempt to injure itself or attract predators. Parents attend to offsprings' demands to reduce the risk.
- Children have motivation to feel negatively towards siblings, as they are co-competitors for limited resources, but also are motivated to have positive regard for siblings as they share 50 % genetic similarity, explaining the contradictory behaviour that siblings display to each other.

- Human parents often demonstrate strategies to cope with sibling rivalry by taking them along different developmental paths, maximising each individual's strengths, reducing conflict and creating very different individuals.

Q Outline the relationship between sexual selection and human reproductive behaviour. *(9 marks)*

C Effects of early experience and culture on adult relationships

1 The influence of childhood experiences on adult relationships

Individuals differ in relationships; some are content in long-term relationships, while others prefer more short-term, less intense associations. Some seem 'lucky in love', while others lurch from one unsuitable relationship to the next. Psychologists have tried to see if the quality and pattern of relationships in adulthood is linked to earlier experiences.

The continuity hypothesis

Bowlby (1951) believed that the type and quality of relationships that individuals have with primary caregivers provides the foundation for adult relationships by creating an *internal working model* which acts as a template for the future. This is the *continuity hypothesis*, the belief that similar relationships will occur as an adult.

Several attachment styles are developed in infancy and these provide children with a set of beliefs about themselves, others and the nature of relationships.

The continuity hypothesis sees attachment types as predicting the nature of adult relationships. Therefore securely attached children have similar relationships throughout life, even with their own children.

Hazan and Shaver (1987) applied Bowlby's theory to adult relationships, arguing that early attachment patterns affect three areas of adulthood: romantic relationships, caregiving and sexuality.

Simpson et al. (2007) performed a longitudinal study on a group of individuals from childhood into their twenties. Securely attached individuals were more socially competent, developed secure friendships and had positive emotional experiences, supporting the hypothesis.

McCarthy (1999) found that women with insecure-avoidant attachments in childhood did not have successful later romantic relationships, while those with insecure-resistant attachments had poor friendships. Those with secure early attachments had successful romantic relationships and friendships, in line with the hypothesis.

- Attachment types are not as fixed as first thought. Hamilton (1994) found that securely attached children could become insecure as a result of life events.
- The temperament hypothesis sees the quality of adult relationships as being determined biologically from innate personality, suggesting that attempts to develop better-quality relationships by changing people's attachment styles to more positive ones would not work.
- Although research shows a link between childhood attachment styles and adult relationships, there may be other factors contributing, so we cannot establish a causal link.

Interactions with peers

Relationships with peers influence later adult relationships. Peers become more influential in adolescence, playing a role in individuals becoming independent adults, helping to develop social skills, including those needed for adult relationships.

Peer relationships do not replace adult attachments; they are just another type of attachment.

Peer relationships differ from adult attachments, as they are horizontal relationships between individuals of equal status.

Adolescent peer relationships develop in two stages. First, friendship cliques form of the same sex around 12 years of age. At age 14, several cliques of both sexes merge to form groups. From these groups, individuals form into romantic couples.

Collins and Van Dulmen (2006) found that experiences in early relationships with parents and peers influence the quality of young adult romantic relationships, offering opportunities to learn expectations, skills and behaviours affecting relationship quality.

Meier et al. (2005) found that the type and quality of adolescent relationships relates to the type and quality of adult relationships, suggesting a link.

Connelly and Goldberg (1999) found that the level of intimacy in peer relationships laid the foundations for the degree of intimacy in young adult relationships.

- Hartup (1993) reports difficulties in calculating the impact of children's peer relationships on adult relationships, as there is a need to differentiate between having friends, who the friends are and the quality of friendships.
- Attachment theories are deterministic in perceiving childhood/peer attachments as causing adult relationships. However, other factors may play a role, such as the different attachment styles people bring to relationships

Furman (1999) believes that because peer relationships are on equal footings, they provide opportunities for cooperation and mutual altruism not present in child–adult relationships and these qualities are important in forming successful romantic relationships.

Q **(a)** Outline one theory that explains the dissolution of relationships. *(5 marks)*
 (b) Outline and evaluate research in to the effects of adolescent experience on
    adult relationships. *(20 marks)*

2 *The nature of relationships in different cultures*

There are differences between cultures in how relationships are formed and undertaken. In Western cultures, partners freely select one another and relationships are ended when one or both partners wish it. In collectivist cultures, where society is seen as more important than individual needs, relationships are more permanent and often arranged by outside parties. Arranged marriages are the commonest form of marriage, with parents being influential in partner choice and subsidiary roles being played by other family members and friends. Relationships in collectivist cultures are more a union between families than individuals. The idea behind arranged marriages is that young people otherwise choose partners on the basis of attraction, which is not perceived as a recipe for success. In two-thirds of the world, a man, or his family, must pay a dowry for his bride; in return, he gets her labour and childbearing qualities.

In multicultural societies, such as the UK, tensions and conflicts occur, with young people valuing individual choice more, and older generations favouring traditional arranged marriages.

Mwamwenda and Monyooe (1997) found that 87% of Xhosa students in South Africa supported the dowry system, seeing it as a sign of the groom's appreciation for his bride.

McKenry and Price (1995) reported that in cultures where females have become more independent and influential, divorce rates have risen, suggesting that lower divorce rates seen in non-individualistic cultures are a reflection not of happy marriages, but of male dominance.

Umadevi et al. (1992) looked at female preferences for love marriages and arranged marriages in India. Arranged marriages were seen positively if the two intended partners consented. However, love marriages were liked too, if there was parental approval, demonstrating the importance of whole family opinions in Indian society.

Zaidi and Shuraydi (2002) interviewed Muslim women of Pakistani origin, raised in Canada, about attitudes towards arranged marriages. The majority preferred love marriages of their choice, although elders, especially fathers, were opposed, showing the potential for discord within cultural groups that form minorities within more dominant cultures.

- The occurrence of totally arranged marriages, where intended partners have no say in the matter, is rare. Most partners in arranged marriages have a right to consent and the majority meet each other at social functions or through a third party.
- Xioahe and Whyte (1990) found contradictory evidence suggesting that arranged marriages are superior to love marriages over time. In China, women reported love marriages more satisfactory than arranged marriages. However, women in China have developed more freedom and influence, and findings may be an expression of this.
- The dowry system has a protective value for women, as husbands may be reluctant to abuse wives they have paid money for. However, it is also used to justify children remaining with the husband's family in the event of divorce, the children having been 'paid for'.
- When researching into cultural differences, cultural bias can be problematic where researchers interpret observations in terms of their cultural norms, such as using measuring tools or questionnaires devised in one particular culture.

Q Discuss research into cultural differences in relationships. *(25 marks)*

A Social psychological approaches to explaining aggression

1 Social psychological theories

Social learning theory

Social learning theory sees aggression as learned in two ways, both involving operant conditioning:
- *Direct reinforcement* — behaviours are reinforced, making them likely to be repeated.
- *Indirect reinforcement* — observed behaviours that are reinforced, observed and imitated (*vicarious learning*).

Through social learning, humans learn the value of aggressive behaviour and how and when to imitate specific acts of aggression.

Although models are necessary for imitation, good levels of *self-efficacy* (situation-specific confidence) are also required.

Media influences form the basis of much research, where it is been found that if observers identify with the perpetrators of aggressive acts and/or the more realistic or believable acts of aggression are, the more likely they will be imitated. However, if perpetrators of aggressive acts are punished, it decreases the chances of the behaviour being imitated.

Bandura et al. (1961, 1963) showed children scenarios involving aggression to a Bobo doll, finding that they imitated behaviours they had observed when allowed to play with the doll. Aggression was imitated more if the model was reinforced, but decreased if the model was punished, suggesting that although observational learning can occur, imitation only happens if the behaviour is vicariously reinforced. Aggression was more likely if a child identified with the model or had low self-esteem

Cooper and McKay (1986) found that after 9 and 10 year-old children had played aggressive video games, acts of aggression increased in girls, but not in boys, suggesting a gender difference.

- There are methodological issues with Bandura's research: Bobo dolls are not real, do not retaliate and are designed to be hit. Johnston et al. (1977) also stated that children who behaved aggressively were rated by their teachers as naturally aggressive, suggesting that personality factors were more important than social learning. There are also ethical considerations in encouraging children to be aggressive.
- Social learning theory does not account for emotional factors in aggressive behaviour.
- Social learning can be seen as stronger than biology, because there are non-aggressive societies, such as the Amish communities in the USA.
- Social learning theory explains individual differences and cultural differences in aggression as resulting from different learning experiences.

Deindividuation

Losing a sense of individual identity deindividuates people. Individuals normally refrain from aggression because they are identifiable, but in situations such as crowds, social restraints and personal responsibility are less and so aggression occurs.

The normative view sees deindividuation as causing people unquestioningly to follow group instead of personal norms, sometimes leading to aggression.

Zimbardo sees people in crowds as anonymous, with lessened awareness of individuality and reduced sense of guilt or fear of punishment, and the bigger the crowd, the more this is so.

Prentice-Dunn and Rogers (1982) believe that individuals normally have awareness of personal moral codes, but being in a crowd diminishes private awareness and so they follow group norms.

Zimbardo (1963) replicated Milgram's electric shock study, with the 'teacher' either individuated with a nametag, or deindividuated by wearing a hood. Hooded teachers gave more shocks, supporting the idea of deindividuation.

Watson (1973) conducted a cross-cultural study, finding that warriors who disguised their appearance with face paint were more aggressive. This suggests that deindividuation effects are universal.

Malmuth and Check (1981) found that a third of US male university students would rape if they could not be identified.

Silke (2003) found that people in disguise perpetrated most assaults in Northern Ireland. The more severe the assault, the more likely the attacker was disguised, suggesting that disguises deindividuate people, reducing guilt and fear of punishment.

- Deindividuation in crowds can also lead to increased pro-social behaviour, as in religious gatherings.
- Deindividuation is used to explain football hooliganism. However, Marsh et al. (1978) found that mainly ritualised behaviour occurred, actual violence being rare.
- Research fails to take into account whether it is the anonymity of the victims of the aggressors, or the aggressors themselves, that leads to aggression.
- One practical application arising out of an understanding of deindividuation is closed-circuit television cameras, such as at football matches, which have reduced violence levels.

Q **(a)** Outline two social psychological theories of aggression.   *(9 marks)*
   (b) Evaluate one theory outlined in (a).   *(16 marks)*

2 Explanations of institutional aggression

Institutional aggression occurs in two ways:
- *Instrumental aggression.* Institutional groups sharing a common identity, such as the army, use aggression in non-emotive ways, as a calculated means of achieving goals.
- *Hostile aggression.* People living in institutions, such as jails, use aggression emerging from emotional states, such as frustration.

Institutional aggression can occur through situational or dispositional (personality) factors.

Warfare. This involves instrumental aggression occurring mainly through situational factors.

Warfare is not uniquely human. Ant colonies wage war and research into warfare among animals led to evolutionary explanations, which see warfare arising from carnivores' hunter-killer instincts, or from group defence behaviour against predators.

Human warfare can be destructive because aggression is not face-to-face, divorcing humans from the consequences of their actions. Opponents are dehumanised, so it is easier to aggress against them, and armies deindividuate soldiers by the use of uniforms.

Kruuk (1972) reported that spotted hyenas wage war over territorial issues and kill other hyenas hunting prey on their territory, suggesting that warfare arises out of group defence mechanisms.

Goodall (1986) reported that groups of chimpanzees will wage war on other groups in order to kill and eat them, suggesting that warfare evolved out of group hunting skills.

- Ardrey (1961) believes that human warfare arises out of the evolution of group hunting skills to catch prey animals.
- Ehrenreich (1997) argues that warfare arose from humans collectively protecting themselves from attackers and the perception of threatened attack. The American 'Indian Wars' can be interpreted as early settlers wiping out indigenous peoples because they were perceived as potential attackers.

Terrorism. The causes of terrorism lie in cultural and sub-cultural clashes, but can be seen as a form of minority influence, where minority groups seek to effect social change by altering majority views. Behaviour and beliefs are consistent and persistent, leading to gradual changes in public opinion.

Terrorism justifies aggression through 'collective responsibility', such as the targeting of random civilians by suicide bombers.

Ministry of Defence Report (2005) found that the majority of Iraqis privately, but not publicly, supported the terrorist insurgency, reinforcing the view that terrorism is a form of minority influence.

Barak (2004) reported that terrorists are generally people exhibiting suppressed anger who have experienced economic and political marginalisation, suggesting that terrorism has its roots in cultural and sub-cultural clashes.

- The idea that terrorism results from experiencing economic and political marginalisation is arguable, as many terrorists, such as the Baader-Meinhof gang, were university educated and from affluent families.
- The idea that there is a 'typical' terrorist is simplistic. It is more probable that a range of explanations are needed to explain the variety of terrorist groups and actions, including instrumental and hostile acts, and encompassing situational and dispositional factors.

Prisons. Zimbardo's prison study was motivated by reported abuses by prisoners and guards, seen as due to dispositional factors. Zimbardo concluded that the behaviour within his prison resulted from situational factors and that brutalising environments produce brutality, suggesting that potential for such behaviour is within us all.

Abuses of Iraqi prisoners by American troops can similarly be explained as resulting from situational factors and not the personalities of the perpetrators, although other factors play a role, such as retaliatory humiliation. Moreover, abuses were committed by low-ranking soldiers under no supervision from officers and may have been an attempt to create status and power.

Haslam and Reicher (2006) found that the BBC prison study (based on Zimbardo's study) could not explain behaviour as due to allotted roles, behaviour being better understood in terms of social identity theory, which sees behaviour as due to in-group and out-group reference points.

Johnston (1991) found that prison overcrowding leads to aggression, due to competition for resources and the adoption of defensive behaviours, either individually or through prison gangs with extreme in-group/out-group beliefs. This suggests situational factors at play.

- The best way to view the debate is from an interactionist viewpoint, personality and situational factors acting upon each other, determining levels and types of aggression.
- Research permitting, an understanding of aggression could lead to practical applications, such as prison reform. Zimbardo's research led initially to changes in the prison system. However, Zimbardo feels that prison regimes became worse, suggesting that his research was not justifiable in cost–benefit terms.

Q Discuss explanations of institutional aggression. *(25 marks)*

B Biological approaches to explaining aggression

Biological explanations view aggression as having internal physiological causes rather than external social or environmental ones. Research concentrates on several biological areas, including genetics, hormones, neurotransmitters and brain structures. Biological factors can be perceived as sole causes or as working in conjunction with other factors.

1 *Neural and hormonal influences*

Neurotransmitters and hormones play important roles in many areas of human functioning. The neurotransmitter *serotonin*, along with hormones such as *testosterone* and *adrenaline*, and the female hormones *oestrogen* and *progesterone*, are involved with aggression.

Serotonin. This is linked with various bodily effects, such as sleep, but low levels of the neurotransmitter are especially associated with increased levels of aggression (and high levels with reduced aggression).

Delville et al. (1997) found that drugs increasing serotonin production lead to reduced levels of aggression, suggesting that low levels of serotonin are linked to increased aggression.

Popova et al. (1991) found that animals selected for domesticity because of reduced aggression levels had lower serotonin levels than wild, more aggressive counterparts.

Linnoila and Virkunen (1992) found a relationship between low levels of serotonin and violent behaviours, suggesting that a lack of serotonin is linked to aggression.

Lidberg et al. (1985) compared serotonin levels of violent criminals with non-violent controls, finding the lowest levels of serotonin among violent criminals.

- Various drugs are associated with reducing serotonin levels and increasing aggression. Penttinen (1995) reports cholesterol-lowering drugs such as lopid, appetite suppressors such as fenfluramine and even low-fat diets produce such effects. Some drugs have been withdrawn because of their anti-serotonergic effects.
- Huber et al. (1997) argues that reducing serotonic activity in a wide range of species, from crustaceans to humans, increases aggression, suggesting an evolutionary link.
- Evidence linking low levels of serotonin and aggression is only correlational and does not indicate causality.

Testosterone. This is a male hormone associated with aggression, and more associated with males. Castration, which lowers testosterone levels, reduces aggression.

Testosterone given to females heightens levels of aggression, although effects are not universal, some research not finding links between heightened testosterone levels and aggression.

Testosterone modulates levels of various neurotransmitters that mediate effects on aggression. There seems to be a critical period early in life, where exposure to testosterone is essential to elicit aggression in adulthood. It is thought that testosterone helps to sensitise an androgen responsive system (responsive to male hormones).

Higley et al. (1996) reported that individuals with elevated testosterone levels exhibit signs of aggression, but rarely commit aggressive acts, suggesting that social and cognitive factors play a mediating role.

Edwards (1968) found that giving testosterone to neonate female mice made them act like males with increased aggression, when given testosterone as adults. However, control females only given testosterone as adults did not react in this way, suggesting that testosterone masculinises androgen-sensitive neural circuits underlying aggression in the brain.

Bermond et al. (1982) found that testosterone affects certain types of aggression in animals, such as intermale aggression as a defence response to intruders, while predatory aggression is not affected.

- Castration research indicates reduced aggression. However, castration disrupts other hormone systems too, and these may be playing a part. One problem with studying animals is that certain brain structures are involved with different types of aggression in different species, creating problems in trying to generalise to humans.
- Results from human studies are often subjective, relying on questionnaires and observations.

Q   Outline and evaluate the role of neural and hormonal mechanisms in aggression.

(25 marks)

2   The role of genetic factors in aggressive behaviour

Research indicates various genes associated with aggression. The MAOA gene, which helps to eliminate excess amounts of neurotransmitters, such as serotonin and dopamine, is implicated, as well as the sex chromosome gene Sry.

Rissman et al. (2006) investigated Sry, a gene leading to the development of testes and high androgen levels in males. Male and female mice with and without the gene were tested, with the Sry gene being associated with high levels of aggression, suggesting that genes and hormones interact and that sex chromosome genes also have a role.

Brunner et al. (1993) studied a family where all the males had a mutant form of the MAOA gene. All reacted aggressively when angry, fearful or frustrated, suggesting that abnormal MAOA activity is associated with aggression.

New et al. (2003) found that acts of impulsive aggression, such as domestic violence, have a genetic component related to the serotonergic system, suggesting that many genes may be involved in aggression.

- One-third of males carry the low-level activity version of the MAOA gene, suggesting that it bestows adaptive advantages. Associated with risk taking, it has beneficial qualities in occupations such as working on the stock market.
- Generalising from animals to humans is problematic, as similar results are not always found: for example, mice lacking the HTR1B gene, associated with serotonin production, have elevated levels of aggression, but humans do not.
- Drug treatments may be possible for people with the low-level activity version of the MAOA gene to help control aggressive urges. However, drug treatments have so far not had success in controlling aggression, suggesting that other non-biological factors may be involved.

Brain structures

Various brain structures are associated with aggression, with the cortex playing an inhibiting role over the sub-cortical limbic system, preventing aggression. The amygdala is seen as having an important role too.

Research into violent criminals links abnormalities in their limbic systems to murderous behaviour, and tumours within the limbic system have elicited aggression.

Bard (1929) removed the cortex from cats' brains, eliciting anger without emotional content ('sham' rage), suggesting that the cortex plays an inhibitory role over the limbic system, regulating aggression.

Raine et al. (1997) scanned murderers' brains, finding abnormalities in their limbic systems more likely. This suggests that the limbic system is involved in the control of aggression.

Egger and Flynn (1967) found that stimulating one area of the amygdala produces an inhibitory effect, but lesioning it creates increased aggression, suggesting that the amygdala plays a role in regulating aggression.

- The relationship of the limbic system to aggression is a complex, with different areas being implicated in different forms of aggression.
- Research linking brain abnormalities to violent crime is correlational and, although having abnormalities may increase individual vulnerability to being aggressive, other factors may be involved.

General evaluation

- Biological explanations can lead to better understanding, allowing development of practical applications for aggressive behaviour, such as drug treatments.
- Explanations perceiving biology alone as determining aggression are deterministic, seeing no role for free will. This may be true for lower animals, but human behaviour also involves cognitive inputs.
- Biological explanations cannot explain cultural differences in types and levels of aggression, although they can suggest explanations for differences between men and women.

Q Compare social and biological approaches to explaining aggression.   *(25 marks)*

C Aggression as an adaptive response

1 *Evolutionary explanations of human aggression*

Aggression is seen as having an adaptive advantage, becoming widespread through natural selection.

Lorenz (1966) saw aggression as an instinct, which evolved into rituals, such as males' dominance fights, protecting animals from incurring harm, one animal generally backing down.

Recent evolutionary theories see aggression as a means of solving adaptive problems over a wide range of behaviours, between and within species.
- *Between species.* Prey animals use aggression to defend themselves and their offspring. Prey animals have evolved the ability to gauge the strength of predators; therefore the 'flight or fight' response is dependent upon this calculation. Altruistic alarm calls to the presence of predators have also evolved as a prey defence mechanism.
- *Within species.* Aggression between members of one species serves several purposes, such as establishing dominance hierarchies. Males compete for access to females and so are more aggressive towards one another.

Jealousy. This occurs through fear of losing affection or status and is characterised by feelings of resentfulness, bitterness and envy. It can motivate aggressive behaviours:
- *Male–male rivalries* — males compete for access to females, often in ritualised ways.
- *Female–female rivalries* — females compete to be attractive and criticise other females' appearances, as males value attractiveness as a sign of fertility.
- *Sibling rivalry* — siblings compete for parental resources to maximise adaptive fitness.

Daly and Wilson (1988) reported that male–male aggressive rivalries are found among young males in most cultures, suggesting that the behaviour is universal as a result of evolution.

Barrett et al. (2002) used Viking blood feuds to show how having aggressive 'berserker' members in a family group benefited survival, suggesting that aggression was naturally selected.

Buss and Dedden (1990) found that females criticise the appearance and sexual promiscuity of other females, suggesting that they are reducing potential rivals' attractiveness and raising their own by doing so, in line with evolutionary theory.

- All researchers do not see predation as aggressive. It lacks an emotional component and areas activated in the hypothalamus during predation are similar to those associated with hunger, rather than aggression.
- Harris (2004) believes that sibling jealousy evolved to maximise parental resources and that this explains the origins of jealousy better than infidelity.
- The tendency towards violent acts over minor territorial disputes between neighbours is explained in evolutionary terms as territorial defensive behaviour involving male–male rivalries.

Infidelity. This is seen in terms of sexual unfaithfulness, but also encompasses emotional loyalty and fidelity.

Evolutionary theory sees cues initiating sexual jealousy as being weighted differently between genders. Males are not sure of paternity and fear indications of sexual infidelity in females, such as smiling at other men, which triggers sexual jealousy and initiates aggression to ensure sole access to his partner. A male's sexual infidelity does not threaten females' certainty of maternity, but the female does fear male emotional involvement with other women where they spend resources on them, which she would prefer to be spent on her and her children. Therefore deprivation of emotional support triggers jealousy in women. Jealousy can also be initiated by the presence of younger, attractive women.

Buss et al. (1992) found that males had higher stress levels when viewing pictures of sexual infidelity, while females had higher levels when viewing pictures of emotional infidelity, suggesting that different environmental cues trigger aggression in males and females.

Looy (2001) found that jealousy in women is triggered by the presence of younger, more attractive women, in line with evolutionary predictions.

Goetz et al. (2008) looked at men's violence against intimate partners and found that violence functions to punish and deter female sexual infidelity, its frequency being related to suspicions of sexual infidelity.

- Harris (2003) found that Buss et al.'s findings about males being more stressed by sexual infidelity and females by emotional infidelity are true of imagined scenarios, but in reality both genders feel threatened by emotional fidelity. The results from imagined scenarios might be explained as males being aroused by images of sexual infidelity, rather than feeling threatened.
- Critics feel that evolutionary explanations justify violence by men against women as natural and inevitable.
- The evolutionary perspective offers an explanation of how aggression due to suspicions of infidelity may arise via natural selection.

Q Outline evolutionary explanations of human aggression. *(9 marks)*

2 *Explanations of group display in humans*

Group displays are ritualised displays of aggression, serving the functions of determining dominance hierarchies in relation to ownership of territory and intimidation of other groups. Sports events include features demonstrating group displays; indeed, many aspects of sport serve as a vehicle for group display, both on and off the pitch.

Lynch mobs are another example of group display, where temporary groups of people are involved in the common pursuit of a violent act.

Sports events

War dances/supporter displays. These are performed before battle to intimidate and motivate. They are incorporated into sporting occasions, serving the same purpose (e.g. the New Zealand haka).

Other sports developed specialist dance troupes to rouse emotional support and intimidate the opposition. Some sports use mascots to the same end and there have been examples of mascots fighting. War dances have been incorporated into supporter displays, such as the wearing of club colours, face painting and club anthems.
- Such displays are motivating and increase social identity.
- *Territorial behaviour* — group displays mark out and defend territories, such as team supporters congregating in traditional areas.
- *Ritual behaviour* — much aggression between rival sports fans is ritualistic, where a lot of posturing and verbal abuse occurs, but little actual violence, suggesting that it is a symbolic show of strength to limit injuries.

Shwarz and Barkey (1977) believe that teams win more games at home due to social support of home supporters, suggesting that territorial group displays are a factor.

Morris (1981) studied Oxford United fans, home and away, finding behaviour territorial and ritualised, which suggests that group displays serve a social purpose.

End (2005) found that the environment of sports events encourages aggressive group displays, suggesting that they are a social construction.

Grieve (2005) believes that identification with teams is psychologically important, suggesting that group displays allow individuals to feel a sense of social identity.

- Marsh (1982) believes that if ritual aggressive practices between fans were curtailed, violence rates would increase.
- Although group displays may be a factor in aggression levels related to sports events, there are other explanatory factors too, including biological and cognitive ones.
- The universal nature of war dances cross-culturally in sport suggests that the behaviour may have an evolutionary component related to ritualised aggression.
- Many sports teams' war dances are artificial, constructed for commercial purposes, and do not reflect traditional practices.

Lynch mobs

Lynch mobs are associated with unlawful group action resulting in death. Such behaviour was described by Le Bon's (1903) *contagion theory* as irrational, unthinking, characterised by anger and occurring as a result of *deindividuation*, where an individual loses their sense of identity. Mob behaviour was seen as a social contagion spreading quickly, turning crowds into collections of people indulging in unconscious acts of violence.

Convergence theory sees crowd behaviour as constructed by particular individuals within a crowd. Crowd behaviour is seen as a convergence of similarly minded people, so lynch mobs are seen as occurring because of popular, deep-seated hatred of those being lynched.

Turner and Killian's (1957) *emergent-norm theory* sees crowd behaviour as desired, collective actions of people, directed by norms emerging at the time, with different individuals taking on different roles. This means that crowds can be unpredictable, as norms arise spontaneously.

Aguirre et al. (1998) investigated crowd behaviour during an explosion at the World Trade Center in 1993, finding behaviour consistent with emergent-norm theory, supporting the theory.

Waddington et al. (1987) compared violent and non-violent miners' rallies, finding that police actions led to violence, which was dependent on the social context, not the characteristics of the crowd.

Berk (1974) found that convergence theory could not explain all crowd behaviour, suggesting that it lacked theoretical structure.

Turner and Killian (1957) reported that not all members of crowds behave in the same way, casting doubt on Le Bon's idea of social contagion.

- Brown and Lewis (1998) applied theories to anti-Vietnam crowds of the 1970s, concluding that no one theory could explain all behaviour, thereby demonstrating the non-universal nature of such crowds.
- The media focus on riotous crowd behaviour, ignoring peaceful crowds, giving the wrongful impression of crowds as contagious mobs.
- Wright (1978) criticised emergent-norm theory as being incomplete and having limited practical applications.
- Research into emergent-norm theory suggests that the theory explains the difference between relatively unpredictable collective behaviour and more predictable institutionalised behaviour.

Q Outline and evaluate explanations of group displays of aggression in humans.

(20 marks)

5 Eating behaviour

A Eating behaviour

1 Factors influencing attitudes to food and eating behaviour

Eating is necessary to survival. Many factors influence attitudes to food and eating, the three prime ones being mood, cultural influences and health concerns. Sensory qualities are influential too, through either learning or an innate basis. Information about food helps to form expectations and affects behaviour. Social environment can also directly or indirectly have an influence. Individual differences are a mediating factor too.

Mood. Emotional states affect eating practices, either in small ways or in ways that can explain abnormal eating practices, such as binge eating.

Wansink et al. (2008) offered popcorn and grapes to participants, finding that people watching a sad film ate more popcorn to try and cheer themselves up, while those watching a comedy ate more grapes to try and prolong their mood.

Wolff et al. (2000) found that female binge eaters had more negative moods on binge-eating days than female normal eaters, suggesting that negative moods are related to abnormal eating.

Cultural influences. Different cultural and sub-cultural groups have different eating practices, transmitted to group members, usually via reinforcement and social learning. Cultural attitudes to the health concerns of food and eating also vary. Culture influences behaviour directly, but more usually has a moderating role on other variables to determine individual eating practices.

Stefansson (1960) reported on the Copper Eskimos who lived on flesh and roots. When given sugar it disgusted them, suggesting that sweet tastes are not necessarily universal to all cultures.

McFarlane and Pliner (1987) found that only sub-cultural groups who consider nutrition to be important prefer healthy food. But this is mediated by socioeconomic factors — if healthy food is expensive, low-income groups will not eat healthily.

Health concerns. The desire to eat nutritious food and avoid an unhealthy diet affects attitudes and behaviour. There are differences between individuals and cultural groupings.

Monneuse et al. (1991) found that people with preferences for high sugar content in dairy products chose items with lower sugar content, suggesting that health concerns do affect eating behaviour.

Tuorila and Pangborn (1988) found that women had intentions to eat healthily, but that actual consumption of dairy products and high-fat foods was based more on sensory qualities of food, showing that attitudes do not necessarily reflect behaviour.

Steptoe et al. (1995) ranked factors taken into account when selecting food. Sensory qualities were ranked highest, above health concerns, indicating that healthy eating is not the most important factor in determining behaviour.

Several other factors mediate food-related attitudes and behaviour.

Sensory qualities. The shape, smell, taste, etc. of food has an influence over whether it is eaten.

Hetherington and Rolls (1996) found that if sensory qualities of a food were perceived negatively, it would not be eaten.

Social environment. Eating rate, style and amount are affected by social environment either directly (e.g. by the presence of others) or indirectly (e.g. by local culinary traditions).

De Castro (1991) found a social facilitation effect, in that the presence of others made people eat more.

Personality. Different personalities are attracted, or not, to different types of food and eating behaviour.

Stone and Pangborn (1990) reported that sensation-seeking personalities are drawn towards stimulating and hazardous eating behaviours, and that neophobics (people who fear anything unknown) are reluctant to eat novel foodstuffs.

Information. A mediating factor on eating behaviour, especially relating to health concerns, is the effect information can have.

Martins et al. (1997) found that information on the health qualities of food has positive, negative or neutral effects, dependent upon the types of food being portrayed, the way the information is presented, and individual attitudes and expectations towards foods.

General evaluation

- Research on mood states suggests that comfort foods should display nutritional information to stop depressed people eating badly; such habits can contribute to people becoming bulimic.
- Research findings could be used to create eating programmes that shape and maintain healthy dietary practices, such as the way information about healthy eating is presented and which groups are targeted.
- For a fuller understanding of the area, both nurture and nature need to be considered: that is, the effects of learning experiences and innate food preferences.

Q Outline factors influencing attitudes to food and eating behaviour. *(5 marks)*

2 *Explanations for the success or failure of dieting*

Dieting is a form of restrained eating involving voluntary restriction of food intake. Dieting is not a modern behaviour; the ability to diet bestowed an adaptive value in times of food shortages. There is a need for successful forms of dieting, as obesity is widespread. Wing and Hill (2001) defined success as 'successful long-term weight loss, involving the intentional loss of at least 10% of initial body weight and keeping it off for at least one year'.

Explanations for the success and failure of dieting involve biological and psychological factors. These should be considered in conjunction with each other rather than as individual explanations. Dieters differ in the extent to which eating is restrained and for how long, and these factors also affect success levels.

Explanations for success

Success is related to being taught skills useful for weight maintenance, rather than just how to lose weight.

Relapse prevention. This is a means of achieving stable energy balance around a lower weight. It involves identifying situations in which 'lapses' occur and how to 'refocus' if they do.

Motivation. This is a factor in determining success. Financial incentives act as a form of positive reinforcement and use of social networks is beneficial in getting others to provide support. Role models can be provided and creating a positive social identity is crucial for success.

Goal setting. This is a motivational factor, dependent on setting achievable targets, with the goal-setting process consisting of short-term goals leading to the long-term goal. Initial targets are easy, increasing confidence and motivation, and dieters are involved in target setting to create a sense of 'ownership'.

Successful dieters share common behaviours promoting weight loss and its maintenance. If weight loss is maintained for 2 years, the chances of long-term success increase dramatically.

Thomas and Stern (1995) found that financial incentives did not promote significant weight loss or help to maintain weight loss, going against the idea of such incentives being a useful motivational tool.

Miller-Kovach et al. (2001) reported social support methods that WeightWatchers offer are superior to individual dieting regimes.

Bartlett (2003) found that dieting success occurs with a reduction of between 500 and a 1,000 calories a day, supporting the idea that achievable goal setting is a motivational force.

Wing and Hill (2001) reported that low-fat diets, constant self-monitoring of food intake and weight, and increased physical activity lead to successful weight loss.

Explanations for failure

Diets fail as they are unsustainable — initial weight loss slows and weight is regained. The more restrictive the diet, the more likely it will fail. A prime factor is a lack of knowledge and skills necessary to diet sensibly. Unpleasant side-effects, such as stress, create motivational loss and abandonment. Dieters perceive dieting as a temporary restriction, then return to old eating habits and regain weight.

The hormone ghrelin plays a biological role, stimulating appetite, making hungry people even hungrier during dieting and increasing the chances of abandonment. Cognitive factors play a role too, with a lessening of concentration associated with failure.

Jeffery (2000) found that obese people start regaining weight due to a failure to maintain behavioural changes, suggesting that loss of motivation and social pressure have negative influences.

Cummings et al. (2002) found that low-calorie diets stimulate appetite by increasing ghrelin production, reducing the chances of losing weight. The success of stomach-reduction surgery may be due to smaller stomachs producing less ghrelin.

Williams et al. (2002) found that people lacking concentration are unsuccessful, as they lose focus on targets and strategies, indicating cognitive factors to be important.

Evaluation

- Individual differences contribute to success rates. 'Low-restrainers' find dieting easy, while 'high-restrainers' find it difficult. Mensink et al. (2008) think high-restrainers are hypersensitive to food cues, and thus likely to abandon diets. Stirling et al. (2004) found that high-restrainers could not resist forbidden chocolate. However, it is not known whether being a high- or low-restrainer is innate or learned.
- Research findings may lead to strategies for successful dieting that successfully treat obesity.
- Nolen-Hoeksema (2002) found that females on low-fat diets develop negative moods and so overeat, with 80% developing depression. This suggests that dieting leads to mental disorders. Perhaps low-fat dietary products should display warnings about such risks.

Q Discuss explanations for the success and/or failure of dieting. *(25 marks)*

B Biological explanations of eating behaviour

1 The role of neural mechanisms

Various neural mechanisms are linked to the control of eating. The hypothalamus is regarded as the hunger centre of the brain, with the ventromedial and lateral hypothalamus featuring in *dual control* and *set-point* theories. Other limbic system areas play a part, indicating the complexity of biological factors in hunger and satiation. Hormonal factors also play a role.

The hypothalamus. This is part of the limbic system, linking the nervous system to the endocrine system and acting like a thermostat to initiate or stop eating behaviour.

Dual control theory (DCT). This has a *homeostatic* view of hunger and satiety. When glucose levels fall, the *lateral hypothalamus* (LH) is activated, causing the sensation of hunger and motivating a person to eat, which releases glucose. This activates the *ventromedial hypothalamus* (VMH), leading to a feeling of satiety, and eating stops.

> **Hetherington and Ranson (1940)** found that lesions to the VMH lead to overeating and weight gain. **Anad and Brobeck (1951)** found that lesions to the LH lead to undereating and weight loss, supporting DCT.
>
> **Stellar (1954)** found that stimulating the VMH decreases eating, but when lesioned, increases eating; while the LH, when stimulated and lesioned, produces the opposite effects, supporting DCT.

- Leisioned VMH rats overeat and gain weight. However, this is temporary and body weight stabilises. DCT cannot explain this as leisioned VMH rats are achieving satiety, even though their satiety centre is supposedly absent.
- Lesioned LH rats will not eat or drink and lose weight. However, these effects are temporary and eating ability is regained, even though they have supposedly lost their hunger centre. DCT cannot explain this.

Set-point theory (SPT). This was a solution to explaining the long-term effects of lesioning the VMH and LH, with the VMH and LH perceived as controlling body weight by a set-point mechanism. Lesioning the LH lowers the set-point for body weight, with body weight being maintained at a lower level than before. Lesioning the VMH heightens the set-point, body weight being maintained at a higher level than before.

> **Powley and Keesey (1970)** found that rats that lose weight through starvation and then have lesions made to their LH do not lose further weight. This indicates that the rats had slimmed down to a new set-point before the lesions were created, supporting SPT.
>
> **Proc and Frohman (1970)** found that rats made obese through VMH lesioning, then force-fed to increase body weight, lost weight when fed normally, supporting SPT, as the rats returned to their new increased set-point.

- Research indicates the neural mechanisms involved are complex. Ungerstedt (1971) found that lesions to the nigrostriatal tract, an area outside the LH, also produces aphagia.
- Perceiving the VMH as a satiety centre and the LH as a hunger centre is simplistic. Lesions to the LH also produce disruptions to aggression levels and sexual behaviour.

Hormonal factors. These have roles in the control of eating. *Glucostatic theory* sees brain mechanisms as monitoring blood-glucose levels, with glucoreceptors located in the VMH.

Glucose comes from the intestine producing *cholectystokinin*, activating the liver to release glucose and signal the brain. *Lipostatic theory* perceives reduced fat levels as causing hunger. The fat-derived hormone *leptin* lowers activity in brain areas associated with hunger, while heightening them in areas associated with satiety.

Schneider and Tarshis (1995) found that lesioning the LH leads to body weight falling, as stored body fat is released to compensate for less insulin production. As the bloodstream is now energy rich, brain mechanisms believe that eating is not required, suggesting that the LH controls insulin levels.

Pinel (2000) found that lesioned VMH rats have increased insulin levels, causing food to be converted to fat. The rats eat more to address the shortage of glucose, causing weight increase, suggesting that the VMH also controls insulin levels.

- Research has tended to consist of artificial laboratory experiments, where animals are not allowed to eat freely. This suggests that results may not be ecologically valid.
- Cognitive factors also play a role in determining satiety. We are aware that we have eaten, and therefore logically we assume that we are full.

Q Outline the role of neural mechanisms involved in controlling eating and satiation.

(9 marks)

2 *Evolutionary explanations of food preference*

Food preferences have evolved as they have an adaptive value. Most human evolution occurred during the Pleistocene era, a time of nomadic hunter-gatherers, with food only periodically available. Therefore humans evolved to favour energy-rich foods and store excess as fat for times of scarcity. We still exhibit these tendencies, even though food is perpetually available. Food preferences therefore reflect the need for energy, stored nutrition and the necessity to avoid toxins.

Sweet tastes. These are indicative of high-energy and non-toxic content and were acted upon by natural selection to become a universal food preference.

De Araujo et al. (2008) found that mice that could not taste sweetness preferred sugar solutions to non-calorific sweeteners, suggesting that the preference is based not on sweetness, but on calorific content.

- A fondness for sweetness is common in the animal kingdom, lending support to it being an evolutionary preference.

Bitter tastes. These are indicative of toxins. Plants produce toxins to discourage being eaten and therefore it is evolutionarily beneficial to develop an ability to detect and avoid bitter tastes.

Mennella (2008) found children more sensitive to bitter tastes than adults, suggesting an innate preference, with learned preferences overtaking inborn ones over time. This explains why children do not like bitter-tasting vegetables and will not swallow bitter medicines

- A practical application of research is that children's medicines could have sweet tastes added to make them palatable.
- 35% of children (but few adults) have a preference for sour tastes, suggesting that these children are less food neophobic and will sample a greater variety of foods, incurring a selective advantage.

Salty tastes. Without sodium chloride we would dehydrate and die. A high sodium concentration is required in the bloodstream to maintain nerve and muscle activity.

> **Dudley et al. (2008)** found that ants in inland, salt-poor environments prefer salty solutions to sugary ones, seemingly an adaptive response to maintain their evolutionary fitness.
>
> **Beauchamp (1983)** found that people with sodium deficiency have an innate response to ingest salt, finding it more palatable and less aversive at high concentrations than related family members, indicating an evolutionarily determined mechanism to maintain sodium levels.

- There are individual differences in salt preferences, which is puzzling, as evolution would predict a standard universal preference.

Meat. Meat is high in protein and energy-rich fat. Group hunting skills made meat more available and cooking more palatable. Meat has been associated with a growth in human intelligence. Hunting was dangerous and meat eating risky, as meat can be toxic and incur transmittable diseases.

> **Foley and Lee (1991)** compared brain size with primate feeding strategies, concluding that meat eating led directly to the process of encephalisation. This suggests that evolution favoured meat eating in humans.
>
> **Finch and Standford (2004)** believes that meat eating allowed humans to exploit new environments, suggesting an adaptive advantage.

- Kendrick (1980) found that longevity is associated with vegetarianism, suggesting that there is a cost to meat eating.
- Dunn (1990) points out that human dental structures and digestive systems are closer to herbivores than carnivores and that true carnivores eat meat raw, guts and all, suggesting no evolutionary preference for meat eating.

Variety. An innate preference for a variety of foods is beneficial as it increases food supplies, allows variation in times of scarcity and permits ingestion of a wide range of vitamins and minerals.

> **Davis (1928)** found that children prefer a wide range of food, suggesting an evolutionarily determined preference. However, **Sclafani and Springer (1976)** offered a wide range of foods to rats, but they only ate junk foods, becoming obese.

- Having a preference for variety would mean liking new foods that may be poisonous.
- Food neophobia indicates that variety has not been determined by evolution.

Q Outline and evaluate evolutionary explanations of food preferences.   *(25 marks)*

C Eating disorders

Candidates need to have studied at least one eating disorder. This book concentrates on obesity, but other eating disorders would be equally acceptable.

Obesity is defined as a body mass index of 30 kg/m². In 2008, in Britain 24 % of people were obese, and in the USA, obesity is the second biggest cause of preventable death, linked to cardiovascular diseases, diabetes, etc. with 9 % of health costs attributed to the condition. Various factors contribute to obesity and only by gaining insight into the condition can it be addressed.

1 *Psychological explanations of obesity*

Psychodynamic explanation

Obesity is seen as due to unresolved conflicts, such as emotional deprivation during the oral stage, with the libido then becoming locked on to oral gratification. Obesity is also linked to other factors explicable by psychodynamic means, such as depression.

Felliti (2001) reported on five cases of sleep-eating obesity (eating food while asleep). All had suffered abuse in childhood and their behaviour was interpreted as an unconscious anxiety reducer, backing up the theory.

- Most obese people have not suffered abuse and do not indulge in sleep eating, casting doubt on the explanation.
- Obesity is widespread, but there is no evidence of a parallel rise in unresolved childhood conflicts, casting doubt on the explanation.
- Cases of depression etc. linked to obesity could be an effect of obesity rather than a cause.

Behavioural explanations

Obesity is seen as a maladaptive, learned behaviour occurring through overeating in three possible ways:
- *Classical conditioning* — obesity occurs because food is naturally associated with pleasure and food cues come to be associated with the pleasure response.
- *Operant conditioning* — obesity occurs due to food being used as a reinforcer for desirable behaviour.
- *Learning theory* — obesity is seen as caused by the observation and imitation of obese role models.

Jackson (2008) reports that reinforcing children for eating creates a compulsion that can lead to obesity, suggesting that operant conditioning in childhood is to blame.

Hardeman et al. (2000) found that treating obesity by role models encouraging healthy lifestyles led to significant weight loss, lending support to behavioural explanations.

- Operant conditioning techniques have been used to treat obesity by reinforcing healthy practices, but Devlin et al. (1995) found that weight loss was not maintained, suggesting that operant conditioning does not explain the causes of obesity.
- Treatments based on classical conditioning create specific goals and identify clearly what is required. Wing et al. (2002) found that such treatments incur average weight loss of 15.6 kg in 18 months, suggesting that such treatments do work.

Cognitive explanations

Cognitive theories see obesity as occurring through maladaptive thought processes, with information processing having an elevated focus for food-related stimuli.

Braet and Crombez (2001) found that obese children were hypersensitive to food-related words, suggesting an information-processing bias for food stimuli, leading to obesity.

Cserjesi et al. (2007) examined cognitive profiles of obese boys, finding them deficient in attention capabilities, suggesting that childhood obesity involves cognitive deficits.

- Attention deficits may be an effect of being obese. Elias (2003) found that early-onset, long-term obesity leads to a decline in cognitive functioning, weakening the cognitive explanation for obesity.
- The success of therapies based on the cognitive approach suggests that cognitive factors may be involved in developing obesity. O'Rourke et al. (2008) found that cognitive-behavioural therapy significantly improved weight loss.

Q Discuss two or more psychological explanations of one eating disorder.   *(25 marks)*

2 *Biological explanations of obesity*

Genetic explanations

Some individuals may be more genetically predisposed to becoming obese, and having multiple genes linked to obesity increases the chances of the condition developing.

Frayling et al. (2007) found that people with two copies of the fat mass and obesity gene (FTO) had a 70% chance of becoming obese, while those with one copy had a 30% chance, supporting the idea of multiple genes increasing the chances of becoming obese.

Willer et al. (2008) have located new genes associated with obesity, which increase the chances of becoming obese, suggesting that genetics play a role in creating a predisposition to obesity.

- Genes cannot explain the upsurge in obesity. Genes have not changed, but environmental factors, such as the availability of food, have. This suggests that environment plays the larger role.
- Musani et al. (2008) have suggested that obese people may be more fertile, reproduce more and ultimately increase genes favouring obesity in the population.
- The discovery of genes related to obesity may lead to gene therapies for the treatment of the condition.

Neural explanations

The hypothalamus, identified with playing a role in the regulation of eating, is associated with the development of obesity. Specific neural circuits have been investigated, as well as associated hormones and neurotransmitters.

Stice et al. (2008) reports that obese people have fewer dopamine receptors in the brain. They tend to overeat to compensate for having a poorly functioning dorsal striatum, leading to lessened dopamine signalling in the brain. This implies that the neurotransmitter dopamine is linked to obesity.

Reeves and Plum (1969) conducted a post-mortem on an obese female, finding that her VMH had been destroyed. This suggests that the hypothalamus is associated with the development of obesity.

- The evidence linking dopamine to obesity tends to be correlational, so it is not clear if dopamine is a cause or an effect of being obese.

Evolutionary explanations

Human eating habits are more suited to the environment of evolutionary adaptiveness (EEA), where food was not universally available. Humans evolved to find high-calorie foods desirable and to store excess energy as fat for times of scarcity. Humans also evolved to minimise physical activity in order to preserve fat stores. Therefore humans are not suited to a sedentary world of ever-available fatty foods and are vulnerable to overeating foods that were not part of their evolutionary past, because they do not trigger neural mechanisms that control appetite.

The *thrifty gene model* believes there was a selective advantage for people with insulin resistance, as they could metabolise food more efficiently. This was advantageous in times of food scarcity, but now that food is always available, it leads to obesity.

DiMeglio and Mates (2000) found that participants put on more weight when given liquid calories rather than an equal amount of solid calories, supporting the idea that liquid calories have caused the increase in obesity because we are not shaped by evolution to cope with them.

Rowe et al. (2007) studied Pima Indians who have high levels of obesity, concluding that they have a thrifty metabolism allowing them to metabolise food more efficiently. Once an advantage in times of food scarcity, it now leads to obesity, supporting the thrifty gene hypothesis.

- The thrifty gene hypothesis can explain why people who do not have the gene are able to eat lots and not put on weight.
- The evolutionary view offers a plausible explanation for modern levels of obesity and why people find losing weight difficult. Humans are designed to consume as much as possible and lay down fat stores.

Hormonal explanations

An increasing feature of research is what role various hormones play in the development of obesity. *Insulin* has attracted interest for its role in directing the storage and utilisation of energy. *Cortisol* attracts attention due to its powerful metabolic effects. *Ghrelin* has been investigated as its secretion stimulates eating.

Kahn and Flier (2000) found that insulin resistance coupled with a large consumption of high-glycemic foods leads to obesity. Therefore insulin resistance does not seem to be a sole cause.

Epel et al. (2001) found that women with high levels of cortisol overeat sweet foods, suggesting a role for cortisol in developing obesity.

Shintani et al. (2001) found that the action of ghrelin does not have a direct influence, but is caused by the production of leptin, controlled through increased action of the neuron NPY, suggesting neural factors to be important.

- It is not clear whether abnormal levels of cortisol are a cause or an effect of obesity.
- Evidence suggests that hormonal factors play a contributory role in developing obesity rather than being direct causes.

Q Compare psychological and biological explanations of one eating disorder.   *(25 marks)*

6 Gender

A Psychological explanations of gender development

1 Cognitive development theory

The focus is on how children's thinking develops in qualitatively different stages. Gender identity results from a child's active structuring of its own experiences and not as a passive outcome of social learning. Cognitive developmental theory sees thinking and understanding as the basis behind gender identity and gender role behaviour.

Kohlberg sees a child developing gender understanding in three distinct stages, with gender role behaviour apparent after an understanding is reached that gender is fixed and constant. Schema theory believes that a child only needs gender identity to develop gender-consistent behaviours, while Kohlberg sees the acquisition of gender constancy as necessary first.

Gender schema theory shares Kohlberg's cognitive view of gender understanding, but suggests that a child has schemas for gender at an earlier stage.

Kohlberg's theory of gender constancy

Kohlberg's (1966) theory sees gender concepts as occurring through environmental interactions, restricted by cognitive capabilities at a given time. Kohlberg proposed three stages in which a child attains increasingly sophisticated gender concepts, a new stage only appearing after thinking has matured to a certain point. Consequently, children understand gender differently at different ages, with gender concepts developing as children actively structure their social experiences. It is not, therefore, a passive social learning process occurring through observation and imitation.

After *gender consistency* is reached, a child starts to develop gender concepts that suit its own gender.

Kohlberg's stages of gender development

Approximate ages	Stage	Description
2–3 years	Gender identity	Knowing who is a boy and a girl, including self
4–5 years	Gender stability	Knowing that gender is fixed and that boys become men and girls become women
5–7 years	Gender consistency	Knowing that gender is constant regardless of changes (e.g. haircuts, clothes, etc.)

Frey and Ruble (1992) informed children that certain toys were either 'boy' or 'girl' toys. Boys who had achieved gender constancy chose 'boy' toys, even when uninteresting; girls of the same stage exhibited similar tendencies, but to a lesser degree.

Thompson (1975) found that by 2 years of age children could self-label and identify the gender of others. By 3 years, 90% showed gender identity, compared to 76% of 2 year-olds, showing the developmental nature of the concept.

- Kohlberg's theory combines social learning and biological developmental factors to explain how gender development occurs.
- The theory tends to concentrate on cognitive factors and therefore may be overlooking important cultural and social influences, such as parents and friends.
- Children demonstrate and reward gender-appropriate behaviours in peers before they have reached gender constancy, casting doubt on Kohlberg's idea of universal stages of development.

Gender schema theory

According to gender schema theory (Martin and Halverson, 1981; Bem, 1981), children are seen as developing gender concepts by cognitively processing information from social interactions, leading to the construction of gender schemas — organised groupings of related concepts.

Once a child has a basic gender identity, it accumulates knowledge about the sexes and organises this into its gender schema, which influences behaviour. *In-group schemas* form, concerning attitudes and expectations about the same gender, as well as *out-group schemas* about the other gender. This leads to favouring the same gender and actively ignoring the other gender. Toys, games and objects become categorised as boys' or girls' toys. Children now participate in same-sex activities and gender-consistent behaviour begins, with gender stereotypes reinforced due to only being exposed to same-sex concepts through social interactions. The theory predicts that, in addition to the development of gender understanding, there is an increase in sex-specific behaviour.

Masters et al. (1979) found that children aged between 4 and 5 selected toys by their gender (boy/girl toy), rather than by which gender was seen playing with the toy, indicating the formation of gender schemas.

Aubry et al. (1999) found that once a belief had taken hold that an item was for the opposite sex, a reduced preference for that item developed, implying that gender schemas do affect behaviour.

- Gender schema theory offers a plausible compromise between social learning and cognitive developmental theories.
- The theory neglects the influence of biological factors, assuming all gender-orientated behaviour is created through cognitive means.
- The theory explains why children's attitudes and behaviour concerning gender are rigid and lasting. Children focus on anything confirming and strengthening their schemas and ignore behavioural examples that contradict them.

Q Outline Kohlberg's cognitive developmental theory. *(9 marks)*

2 *Explanations for psychological androgyny and gender dysphoria*

Psychological androgyny involves having both male and female characteristics. This is regarded positively, allowing an individual to choose appropriate behaviour: that is, acting masculine in some situations and feminine in others, or blending both together.

Olds (1981) believed that androgyny was a developmental stage reached by only some people. Bem (1983) argued that androgynous individuals have a different cognitive style and adopt behaviours, when necessary, which are independent of gender concepts. Therefore in terms of cognitive schema theory, androgynous people are *gender aschematic*, in line with Old's explanation, as an individual only becomes androgynous when they perceive the world without gender stereotypes.

Orlofsky (1977) sees androgyny as a behavioural style learned by reinforcement, allowing individuals to acquire masculine and feminine qualities applicable to different situations. Therefore, androgyny is seen more in behavioural than cognitive terms.

Peters and Cantrell (1993) found that androgynous females had the best quality of relationships, supporting the idea of androgyny being a positive condition.

Kurdek and Siesky (1980) found that androgynous characteristics were seen positively in the workplace, again suggesting that it is a positive condition.

Burchardt and Serbin (1982) found that being androgynous scores well in mental health terms, with typically lower levels of depression, although masculine personalities scored equally well.

- Androgyny is not always a positive trait; individuals may exhibit negative masculine and/or feminine behaviours in a given situation.
- Androgyny is perceived as being psychologically healthier, but Whitley (1988) found that having a traditional masculine identity led to higher self-esteem than being androgynous.
- Old's explanation that androgyny is a higher stage of development fails to explain how or why this occurs in certain individuals.

Gender dysphoria

Gender dysphoria is a psychiatric disorder, affecting males more, which occurs when an individual wishes to change their biological gender. Indications of the condition occur fairly early, with children unhappy wearing clothes of their biological gender, or playing gender stereotypical games. Later behaviour may involve assuming the gender role of the desired sex. Masculinising or feminising hormones can be taken to alter physical features, the ultimate remedy being gender-reassignment surgery.

Psychological explanations centre on maladaptive learning experiences, maladaptive cognitive processes and psychodynamic fixations occurring in childhood development. Biological explanations are increasingly favoured, centring on the idea of an individual's genetic sex not matching their gender. This is seen as occurring during pregnancy, through additional hormones present in the mother, or by insensitivity to the mother's hormones (androgen insensitivity syndrome), leading to the development of female genitals, but with male genes.

Rekers (1995) reported no evidence of dysphoric boys showing evidence of biological causes, but there was a common factor of a lack of stereotypical male role models, suggesting a psychological cause.

Hare et al. (2009) found a relationship between gender dysphoria and variants of the androgen receptor gene, implying that the gene may be involved in a failure to masculinise the brain during development in the womb, supporting a biological explanation.

- Identification of genes possibly associated with the condition has caused concerns about foetal gene screening, with a view to aborting 'at-risk' pregnancies.
- Research in this area is often dependent on case studies, but such a method is often affected by memory bias and selective recall.
- Individuals with the condition often do not perceive it as a disorder, but believe that gender characteristics are a social construction with no relation to biological sex.
- Although gender confusion in childhood can indicate gender dysphoria, only a minority will exhibit the condition into adulthood.

Q **(a)** Outline research into psychological androgyny.   *(5 marks)*
   (b) Outline and evaluate explanations of gender dysphoria.   *(20 marks)*

B Biological influences on gender development

1 The role of hormones and genes

Many physical and behavioural differences between males and females are biological ones. Biological sex is determined by the sex chromosomes X and Y, with an XX combination for a female and an XY combination for a male. Sex chromosomes contain genetic material that controls development as a male or female; during this process sex hormones are produced, which direct sexual development. The SRY gene on the Y chromosome controls whether gonads become ovaries or testes; only if the gene is present will testes appear. Testes produce hormones called androgens, preventing development into a female form.

Testosterone is an androgen, which, when released, causes the development of male sex organs and acts upon the hypothalamus; without this the brain would develop as a female type. Testosterone is associated with masculinisation of the brain, such as development of brain areas linked to spatial skills. Similarly, the female hormone oestrogen helps to feminise the brain.

There are differences in the hypothalamus of males and females, with the *sexual diomorphic nucleus* bigger in males. These differences may occur through the action of sex hormones, although this is not a universal view.

During puberty, testes and ovaries play an important part in determining secondary sexual characteristics, distinguishing men from women.

Deady et al. (2006) found a relationship between high testosterone levels in female saliva and a low desire to have a family, suggesting that a female's maternal drive may be linked to hormone levels.

Money and Ehrhardt (1972) found that girls whose mothers took drugs containing androgen during pregnancy exhibited male behaviours, such as playing sports, and an absence of female behaviours, such as playing with dolls, suggesting that male hormones have an influence on gender behaviour.

Koopman et al. (1991) found that mice that were genetically female, but lacked the SRY gene, developed into male mice if the gene was implanted, demonstrating the important role that the SRY gene plays in determining gender.

- If biological factors were responsible for sex differences, it would be expected that these would be apparent from an early age. However, there is little evidence of early behavioural differences between males and females. Therefore differences appearing later may be explicable by social factors.
- Ethical concerns must be considered when performing research on people with abnormal conditions, such as congenital adrenal hyperplasia. Such participants are especially vulnerable to distress and psychological harm. A cost–benefit analysis may decide if such research would be beneficial.

Q **(a)** Outline the role of hormones in gender development.   *(5 marks)*
  (b) Outline and evaluate the role of genes in gender development.   *(20 marks)*

2 Evolutionary explanations of gender roles

Males and females are believed to have evolved different gender role behaviours due to different adaptive pressures.

Mating strategies. Males produce millions of sperm and can fertilise lots of females, incurring little cost to themselves. However, they are not sure of paternity. Females have fewer opportunities to reproduce and incur high costs when they do. However, they are certain of maternity. Therefore men seek to impregnate as many women as possible and women seek genetically fit males to invest resources in them. Aggressiveness occurs between competing males, so they evolved to be bigger and stronger, while females also compete to be seen as attractive.

Pair bonding. Monogamous pair bonding is advantageous. Females get protection and resources, while males ensure sexual fidelity and a level of paternal certainty.

Adaptive advantage of sex roles. The development of sex roles has an adaptive advantage. Men hunted and women, with caring duties, farmed and prepared food, leading to bigger social groups and an ability to avoid starvation.

Gender roles. Women evolved behaviours consistent with nurturing, as they are constrained by child-caring duties, while men evolved behaviours requiring mobility and power, as they possess greater strength.

Holloway et al. (2002) found that human males are 1.1 times bigger than females, but in chimpanzees, where male competition is more intense, males are 1.3 times bigger, supporting the idea of gender size differences being due to evolutionary pressures.

Wood and Eagly (2002) found that a common characteristic of non-industrial societies was men hunting and killing animals and manufacturing tools, while women looked after children, collected and cooked food, suggesting that gender behaviours have their origins in evolution.

Buss (1989) found that cross-culturally females tend to seek males with resources and ambition, while males seek physical attractiveness and desire younger partners, supporting the idea that mating strategies evolved differently between the sexes due to different environmental demands. The idea that men would place more importance on chastity was only supported to a small extent, casting doubt on the explanation.

- Even if gender roles have evolved, it does not mean they have positive outcomes. For example, men can be negatively affected by feelings of jealousy and rejection.
- The evolutionary approach is criticised by some as being deterministic, seeing gender differences as biologically inevitable.
- Evolutionary theory provides a plausible explanation for the physical differences existing between males and females, and why men tend to be more promiscuous and women more choosy in their sexual behaviour.

Q Discuss evolutionary explanations of gender roles. *(25 marks)*

3 *Biosocial approaches to gender development*

Biosocial theory sees gender as determined by both biological and social factors working in conjunction to produce masculine and feminine behaviours and identities. Therefore, gender cannot be explained by biology alone; for instance, psychological androgyny and gender dysphoria indicate that biological sex does not necessarily reflect gender.

Biosocial theory believes that the perceptions of biological sex lead to gender identity and gender role behaviour. A baby is labelled as male or female and this labelling has consequences for how the child is perceived, with boys and girls treated differently — for example, in how they are handled. So gender can be seen as socially constructed and therefore differing across cultures and over time.

While biological explanations see gender behaviours as being due to biology and therefore fixed and constant, the biosocial model sees them as less rigid. This means it is possible for a person to change and develop in ways not confined by traditional views of male and female behaviour and identity.

Wetherell and Edley (1999) found several styles of adult masculinity exhibited by men, such as 'unconventional', 'sporty' and 'new man', indicating that gender role is not fixed exclusively by biology, and supporting the biosocial view that gender behaviour is flexible.

Smith and Lloyd (1978) dressed babies in non-specific gender clothes and labelled them with a boy or a girl's name. It was found that people played with them in different ways according to their gender label, supporting biosocial theory, which sees the gender label directing how the child is perceived and treated.

Bradley et al. (1998) reported on a biologically male boy who had reassignment surgery and was raised as a female. She exhibited some male behaviours as a child, but preferred female company and, as an adult, felt female and was happy that way, implying that biological sex does not determine gender identity.

- The biosocial model is an example of how psychological approaches can work in unison and should, therefore, not be seen as single, exclusive explanations of human behaviour.
- Studies of individuals being given reassignment surgery and raised as the opposite gender to their biological sex often produce contradictory results and may be prone to researcher bias. For instance, Reiner and Gearhart (2003) found that 16 biological males born without a penis, given reassignment surgery and raised as females, exhibited male tendencies, and 10 decided to become male again. Money (1991), however, found 250 cases of people happy with gender reassignment.
- The model sees gender behaviour as not innate and fixed, which means it should be possible to develop gender identity in new and positive ways.

Q Compare Kohlberg's gender development theory and the biosocial approach to gender development. *(25 marks)*

C Social contexts of gender role

1 *Social influences on gender role*

Parents

Parents reinforce children's gender behaviour by their expectations of what is and is not appropriate. Therefore, when a child demonstrates gender-appropriate behaviour, it is reinforced by rewards of praise and attention. Parents act as gender role models too, demonstrating gender-appropriate behaviours to be observed and imitated. Children may, by a gradual process of immersion, take on their parents' own gender schemas.

Eccles et al. (1990) reported that parents encouraged children to play with gender-stereotypical toys, supporting the idea that parents reinforce gender roles.

Fagot and Leinbach (1995) compared children from 'traditional' families, where the father worked and the mother cared for children, with 'alternative' families, where the mother and father shared childcare. The 'traditional' family children displayed more gender role stereotyping and used gender labels earlier, suggesting that parents do act as gender role models.

- Parents have more influence over children's gender concepts and behaviour when children are young, but peers become more important as gender role models in later childhood.

Peers

Peers have a strong social influence by acting as role models, with children more likely to imitate same-sex models. Peers also help to reinforce gender stereotypes: for example, by praising gender-appropriate clothes and ridiculing non-appropriate ones.

Archer and Lloyd (1982) reported that children who played the opposite sex's games were ridiculed by their peers and ostracised, supporting the idea that peers police gender roles.

Lamb and Roopnarine (1979) found evidence of peers rewarding sex-appropriate play in pre-school children and ridiculing sex-inappropriate play, demonstrating the influence peers have in reinforcing gender behaviour.

- Peers may have a stronger role in reinforcing gender roles than parents because peers police gender behaviours: for instance, by ostracising those indulging in non-stereotypical behaviour.

Schools

Schools exert social influences in several ways. First, teachers may moderate parent and peer influences by reinforcing less gender-stereotypical attitudes and behaviour, but they may also enforce gender stereotypes: for example, through separate dress codes for boys and girls. Teaching materials can exert an influence. Primary school teachers are generally female and this may explain why boys do comparatively worse, perceiving learning to be for girls.

In secondary education there is a tendency for men and women teachers to teach gender-stereotypical subjects, such as men teaching maths, and for pupils to regard subjects as 'girl ' or 'boy' subjects. Again these influences are reinforced and policed by parents, peers and teachers.

Renzetti and Curran (1992) report that teachers give reinforcements in the form of praise to boys for instances of 'cleverness', while girls received praise for 'neatness', supporting the view that teachers enforce gender stereotypes.

Colley (1994) found that in secondary schools, pupils tend to view individual subjects as either masculine or feminine, demonstrating that social influences on attitudes and beliefs about gender are apparent in schools.

- Fagot (1995) found that teachers try to reinforce female behaviours in boys and girls, but that only girls learn them, suggesting that cognitive rather than behavioural factors are stronger.

Media

The media have a strong social influence on gender behaviour by portraying gender stereotyping and reinforcing gender-appropriate behaviours and attitudes. This occurs through social learning, where children observe and imitate stereotypical gender models on television and in books, or by cultivation, where the more television is watched, the more children's perception of the world comes to resemble what they see on television.

Leaper et al. (2006) found that cartoons showed males and females in gender-stereotypical ways. Males were more aggressive and females more fearful, showing that there is a wide range of media influences affecting gender development.

Williams (1986) found that children who view lots of television, where the content is gender stereotypical, have more traditional beliefs about gender roles, suggesting that children are acquiring gender beliefs through observation and imitation.

- Media influences on gender development may be exaggerated because much gender development occurs before 4 years of age, when media influences are not great. Later on, media influences probably reinforce existing gender beliefs rather than creating them.

Q Outline one social influence on gender role. *(5 marks)*

2 *Cross-cultural studies of gender development*

The thinking behind cross-cultural studies is that, if similarities were found in gender roles across cultures, this would suggest that they are biological in nature, while if differences were found, it would suggest they were socially constructed.

Barry et al. (1957) looked at which qualities were deemed important for males and females in non-Westernised cultures, finding that nurturing was a dominantly feminine characteristic, while self-reliance was the same for males. These findings reflect those from Western cultures, suggesting a biological basis to gender roles.

Whiting and Edwards (1988) researched into various cultures' gender attitudes and behaviours, finding that it was fairly universal for girls to be encouraged into domestic and child-caring roles, while boys were assigned tasks involving responsibility, such as looking after animals. This suggests that it is the activities they are given to do that are responsible for the differences in gender roles.

Mead (1935) conducted research into gender differences between tribes in Papua New Guinea. With the Arapesh, both males and females exhibited gentle, caring personas, while with the Tchambuli, the men demonstrated female behaviours, while women exhibited traditional male behaviours, and in the Mundugumor, both sexes showed aggressive personalities. This implies that gender roles are socially constructed rather than being biological in nature.

Williams and Best (1990) looked at attitudes to gender roles in different cultures, finding that there was universal agreement across cultures about which characteristics were masculine and which feminine, men being perceived as dominant and independent, and women as caring and sociable. Children from these cultures exhibited the same attitudes, implying that attitudes to gender roles are universal and biological in nature.

- Collectivist cultures hold much clearer views than individualistic cultures about which gender roles are male and female.
- A methodological problem with cross-cultural studies is that it is difficult to obtain identical samples and there can be problems with researcher bias in terms of their own cultural viewpoints.
- Globalisation may be contributing to the lessening of cultural differences and there has been a reduction in the differences between masculine and feminine gender roles, implying that social influences are stronger than biological ones.
- The findings from cross-cultural studies can be related to the nature/nurture debate. If gender roles, behaviours and attitudes are universal, this suggests that they are innate and due to nature, while if cultural differences are found, it is more indicative of nurture influences.
- There is the possibility of researcher bias in interpreting the behaviours exhibited in Mead's study, and she did subsequently change her views, stating that gender behaviours can be biological in nature.

Q (a) Describe two or more social influences on gender role.   *(9 marks)*
(b) Consider the extent to which gender development can be explained in terms of social factors.   *(16 marks)*

A Theories of intelligence

1 *Psychometric theories*

Psychometrics is a scientific branch of psychology seeking to quantify (measure) human qualities. Psychometric theories perceive intelligence as a set of abilities measurable by mental tests, and hold that intellectual differences between individuals can be determined. Psychometric theories differ in the number of basic factors that intelligence is considered to consist of.

Spearman's two-factor model

Spearman believed that there is a common factor that explains why individuals score similarly on tests of different abilities. Using the statistical technique of factor analysis, he identified two basic factors that intelligence tests measure:
- *General intelligence (g)* — an innate factor underpinning all mental abilities, shared by individuals but in differing amounts.
- *Specific abilities (s)* — a factor concerning specific skills that different individuals possess.

Johnson and Bouchard (2005), using factor analysis to investigate the structure of mental ability, found a single, higher-order factor of intelligence, implying that general intelligence does exist and contributes to all forms of intelligence.

Kitcher (1985) found no single measure of intellectual ability, suggesting that general intelligence is a myth.

- Spearman's work inspired focus on and interest in the study of intelligence.
- Spearman's work led to the introduction of factor analysis into psychology, such as in the study of personality.
- Spearman's theory was not widely accepted and multi-factor theories became more popular.

Guildford's structure of intellect model

Guildford (1967) believed that there were 120 separate mental abilities. Using factor analysis, Guildford proposed that intellectual abilities were divisible into five types of operation (the type of thinking being used), four types of content (what is being thought about) and six kinds of product (the type of answer required). He then set out to devise tests to measure each separate ability.

Guildford (1985) reported the creation of tests to measure 70 separate mental abilities. However, scores achieved on these tests were often similar, suggesting that they may be measuring the same ability and so there could be considerably fewer than 120 different mental abilities.

- Intended as a general theory of intelligence, the structure of intellect model has practical applications in personnel selection and placement.
- Spearman used schoolchildren, with widely ranging intellects, while Guildford used college students who have a narrower range of intelligence. This may have contributed to finding different numbers of basic factors.

Information-processing theories

Information-processing theories present a cognitive approach, perceiving intelligence as dependent upon the stages gone through to create a solution to a problem. Intelligence is seen as being constructed of a set of mental representations of information and the set of processes acting upon them, such as speed of processing. Attempts have been made to measure the speed of each step, the assumption being that these processes are sequential. However, some believe that parallel processing may be involved, where more than one process occurs at the same time.

Sternberg's triarchic theory of intelligence

Sternberg (1977) saw 'street smart' intelligence as how well someone copes with their environment and this is not measurable by IQ tests. Sternberg's theory has three facets (sub-theories): *analytical*, *creative* and *practical*.

Analytical intelligence. Similar to the psychometric viewpoint, this is a type of intelligence measured through academic problems, involving three components: *metacomponents*, *performance components* and *knowledge acquisition components*.

Creative intelligence. This deals with the relationship between intelligence and experience. It involves how well a task is performed in regard to a person's level of experience. Experience has two parts: *novelty* and *automation*.

Individuals are not necessarily gifted in both parts of creative intelligence. Creative intelligence is also associated with *synthetic giftedness*, an ability to create new ideas and solve novel problems.

Practical intelligence. This deals with the relationship between intelligence and an individual's external world. It involves the use of three processes: *adaptation*, *shaping* and *selection* to create a 'fit' between yourself and your environment.

Practical intelligence is associated with *practical giftedness*, an ability to apply new ideas and analytical skills to practical situations.

Merrick (1992) used the Cognitive Abilities Self-Evaluative Questionnaire to find individuals with all three types of intelligence detailed by Sternberg, supporting the components of his theory.

Grigorenko et al. (2001) found that teaching methods based on Sternberg's theory were superior to more conventional methods in improving reading ability, lending support to the theory.

- Gottfredson (2003) believes IQ tests do measure 'street smartness', as they predict a high scorer's ability to live longer, have a good job, stay out of jail, etc.
- Gottfredson (2003) criticised the theory for its non-scientific nature, believing Sternberg's component of practical intelligence is not a form of intelligence, but merely task-specific knowledge — skills learned to cope with particular environments.

Case's information-processing theory

Case (1985) was interested in how intelligence develops and was influenced by Piaget's theory of cognitive development. The theory describes how information-processing ability is related to the degree of *M-space* (mental capacity) a person possesses.

Information-processing ability is seen as developing over time due to three factors: *brain maturity*, *cognitive strategies* and *metacognitive skills*.

Chi (1978) found that child chess players using metacognitive skills recalled more positions on a board than adults who did not have the same skills, supporting Case's theory.

- The theory is objective, as it sees intelligence as measurable due to the capacity of M-space being determinable.
- Psychometric theories merely describe intelligence, whereas information processing theories explain how problems are solved by identifying the cognitive processes involved.

Q **(a)** Outline two theories of intelligence. *(9 marks)*

    (b) Evaluate one of the theories outlined in (a). *(16 marks)*

2   *Gardner's theory of multiple intelligences*

Gardner (1983) believes that individuals possess a *cognitive profile* involving different amounts of various kinds of intelligence. The theory is an educational one, as Gardner believes that schools should offer individual teaching programmes fitting each person's cognitive profile and improving their intellectual weaknesses.

Gardner thinks there is a danger, by not acknowledging certain types of intelligence, of undervaluing individuals who possess high levels of ability in those areas. Each person's cognitive profile is seen as based upon eight core types of intelligence.

Eight core types of intelligence

Type of intelligence	Description
Bodily-kinaesthetic	Concerns bodily movements. Learning occurs by physical interaction (e.g. sports players).
Interpersonal	Concerns interactions with others. Learning occurs through group discussion (e.g. managers).
Intrapersonal	Concerns self-awareness. Learning occurs via introspection (e.g. scientists).
Linguistic	Concerns the use of language. Learning occurs by reading and note making (e.g. writers).
Logical-mathematical	Concerns logic. Learning occurs by reasoning and the use of numbers (e.g. engineers).
Musical	Concerns sensitivity to sound and music. Learning occurs by auditory means (e.g. musicians).
Spatial	Concerns vision and spatial judgement. Learning occurs by visualisation and mental manipulation (e.g. architects).
Naturalistic	Concerns the natural world. Learning occurs by sensitivity to nature (e.g. farmers).

Several criteria were used to provide evidence for the existence of each type of intelligence, such as being talented in one type but not another, neurological evidence indicating specialised brain areas and unique developmental trends.

Other types of multiple intelligence have been suggested, such as *existential* (philosophical) and *moral* intelligence.

Marchand (2008) found evidence supporting the idea of a separate bodily-kinaesthetic intelligence. Mud masons in Mali communicated building skills without using words, but by physical repetition. A practical application could be in teaching apprentices.

Turner (2008) provided evidence for the existence of a separate musical intelligence. Teachers used memorable tunes to successfully fit in lyrics representing material being learned.

Traub (1999) reported evidence from neuroscience supporting the idea of each intelligence type having localised function in the brain. Brain imaging and studies of brain-damaged individuals showed different mental activities to be associated with different brain areas, lending support to the theory.

- As no current tests exist that can identify and measure Gardner's intelligence types, they have been accused of being aspects of personality rather than distinct forms of intelligence.
- Musical and bodily-kinaesthetic intelligences have been criticised as being talents rather than types of intelligence.
- Naturalistic intelligence has also been criticised as being more of an interest than a type of intelligence. However, it may be a form of intelligence for cultures where people live closer to nature.

- Kornhaber (2001) believes that the theory matches what teachers experience, in that people think and learn in many ways. This has led to the theory being incorporated successfully into many teaching practices, allowing the development of new methods to meet the range of learning styles that students possess.

Q Outline and evaluate Gardner's theory of multiple intelligences. *(25 marks)*

B Animal learning and intelligence

1 *The nature of simple learning*

Classical and operant conditioning are from the behaviourist tradition, which sees learning occurring as a result of experience via the process of association. In classical conditioning, a *stimulus* becomes associated with a *response*, while operant conditioning involves learning behaviour due to its consequences. Classical conditioning is associated with behaviour not under conscious control, while operant conditioning is associated with voluntary behaviour.

Classical conditioning

Pavlov (1927) noticed that dogs salivated before food was presented due to other environmental features becoming associated with their feeding, such as a food bowl. The dogs had learned to produce a natural reflex (salivation) to a stimulus not normally associated with that response. Pavlov then paired food presentation with the sound of a bell, quickly getting the dogs to salivate to the sound of the bell alone.

Before learning	food (unconditioned stimulus, UCS) → salivation (unconditioned response, UCR)
During learning	food (UCS) + bell (neutral stimulus) → salivation (UCR)
After learning	bell (conditioned stimulus, CS) → salivation (conditioned response, CR)

In a subsequent series of experiments, various features of classical conditioning were illustrated.

Features of classical conditioning

Type of feature	Description of feature
One-trial learning	A form of classical conditioning where just one pairing of an UCS and a CS produces a CR.
First- and second-order conditioning	First-order conditioning involves pairing a CS with an UCS that directly satisfies a biological urge, while with second-order conditioning, the CS is paired with a UCS that only indirectly satisfies the biological urge.
Generalisation	The conditioning process can be generalised by slightly varying the CS to produce weaker forms of the CR.
Discrimination	Discrimination occurs when the UCS is paired with one specific CS and the CR occurs to this pairing only.
Extinction	If the CS is continually given without the presentation of the UCS, the CR grows weaker and then ceases.
Spontaneous recovery	After apparent extinction, if a rest period is given followed by re-presentation of the CS, the CR is revived.

Operant conditioning

Operant conditioning is based upon Thorndike's (1911) law of effect, which sees behaviours resulting in pleasant outcomes as likely to be repeated in similar circumstances, while behaviours resulting in unpleasant outcomes are unlikely to be repeated.

Skinner (1938) built upon Thorndike's work, using a *Skinner box* where animals were rewarded with food pellets for producing desired behaviours. An animal would accidentally produce an action, such as pressing a lever, causing food pellets to be released. Gradually the animal learned to associate the behaviour with the reward and produce the behaviour every time.

There are four possible outcomes of any behaviour:

Positive reinforcement — receiving something pleasant (e.g. food).

Negative reinforcement — not receiving something unpleasant (e.g. not having to do chores).

Positive punishment — receiving something unpleasant (e.g. being grounded).

Negative punishment — not receiving something pleasant (e.g. not being given a promised treat).

Reinforcements increase the chances of a behaviour recurring, while punishments decrease the chances.

The role of learning in non-human animals

Animals use conditioning to learn about their environment and adapt to changing environments. Research has shown that classical conditioning is used by animals to learn whether food sources are safe, although *biological preparedness*, where the tendency to learn associations depends on biological predispositions to do so, also plays a role.

Operant conditioning allows animals to interact with their environment and, by *trial and error learning*, to shape behaviour via reinforcement and punishment processes (e.g. to find food and avoid danger).

> **Baker (1984)** showed how pigeons use trial and error learning to discover how to use landmarks as navigational aids.
>
> **Fisher and Hinde (1949)** found that animals tend to learn behaviours that resemble innate ones. Blue tits seemingly learned by imitation to drink cream from milk bottles, but this artificial behaviour was easily learned, as it resembled their natural behaviour of stripping tree bark.
>
> **Garcia and Koelling (1966)** showed how rats learn taste aversions by classical conditioning. The rats were exposed to radiation, but came to associate the sickness they felt with the taste of their feeding bottle and refused to drink from it.
>
> **Breland and Breland (1961)** demonstrated instinctive drift, where animals revert to natural behaviours. Pigs trained to put tokens in a piggy bank to get rewards, preferred instead to root in the ground with them.

- Although classical conditioning cannot explain how new behaviours arise, operant conditioning, by the use of reinforcement, can — and thus can explain complex behaviours too.
- In addition to classical and operant conditioning, animals also use social learning via observation and imitation.
- Behaviourism does not account for the role of emotional and cognitive factors in determining behaviour.
- Operant conditioning cannot explain latent learning, where learning seemingly occurs without reinforcement. Tolman (1930) showed that rats learned to navigate a maze without being reinforced, but only demonstrated this when given the incentive of a reward.

Q Discuss the role of conditioning in the behaviour of non-human animals.   *(25 marks)*

2 Evidence for intelligence in non-human animals

Intelligence in animals can be seen as a hierarchy of learning processes, species differing in the degree of behaviour learned. Alternatively, intelligence can be seen as the ability to learn and process information. Ultimately, animal intelligence is closely associated with the capacity to survive and reproduce.

Social learning

Social learning refers to behavioural processes affecting what animals learn via social interactions. Several forms have been identified that concentrate on the ability to solve social problems.

Imitation — behaviour is observed and directly copied.

Enhancement — attention is directed to a particular feature of the environment to solve a problem.

Emulation — the consequences of behaviour are reproduced.

Tutoring — a model encourages, punishes or provides behavioural examples, usually at a cost to the model.

Whiten (1999) found that in chimpanzee colonies, different population-specific behaviours arose in using twigs to eat ants, suggesting that such behaviours are learned by direct imitation.

Nagell (1993) suggested that snow monkeys' apparent imitation of washing potatoes was actually due to attention being focused on to the potatoes and the water, enhancing the chances of the skill being learned by trial and error.

Tomasello et al. (1987) found that chimpanzees emulated a model that demonstrated using a rake to get food. The chimpanzees did not imitate the model's particular actions but developed their own technique, suggesting that they were trying to attain the consequences of the behaviour.

Rendell and Whitehead (2001) found that adult orcas act as tutors by delaying the killing and eating of prey, so youngsters may practise their hunting skills.

- Examples of tutoring are disputed. Adult orcas may not be delaying killing in order for youngsters to learn, but may simply be 'playing with their food'.
- Due to subjective interpretation, it is not clear if behaviour arises via imitation or enhancement.
- Social learning may help animals avoid predators and maximise mate selection.

Self-recognition

Self-recognition is associated with possession of a self-concept, necessary for higher levels of intelligence. Research has involved the mirror-test, where animals have dots painted on their heads while anaesthetised. The degree of dot touching, with and without a mirror, is recorded. Great apes, elephants, dolphins and orcas have this ability, together with some less expected species like crows and pigeons.

Prior et al. (2008) marked magpies with either a bright colour or a non-noticeable 'sham' colour, or not at all. Mark-directed behaviour only occurred when brightly marked and in the presence of a mirror, suggesting that magpies can self-recognise.

Gallup (1977) found that chimpanzees and orang-utans can self-recognise using his mirror-test.

- The mirror test may not be a valid measurement of self-awareness for species primarily using senses other than sight.
- Some birds, such as magpies, need to recognise and recall which other birds observed them storing food in order to prevent stealing. They can therefore self-recognise.

▶ Machiavellian intelligence

Intelligent individuals look after their own interests, by using deception or forming coalitions, but without disturbing social cohesion.

Whiten and Byrne (1988) showed how young baboons use deceit to get their mothers to chase adults away from foodstuffs so they may eat them.

Nishida et al. (1992) reported that alpha males do not share food with rivals, but do with non-rivals so they will assist in any power struggles.

- Evidence suggests that Machiavellian intelligence exists in primates, especially those living in large social groups with high social complexity and an ability to memorise socially relevant information.
- The evolution of advanced cognitive abilities necessary for Machiavellian intelligence has not been adequately explained as yet.

Q Outline evidence for intelligence in non-human animals. *(9 marks)*

C The evolution of intelligence

1 Evolutionary factors in the development of human intelligence

Human intelligence is seen as having evolved due to the demands of an ever-changing environment creating selective pressure for increased intellect. Humans needed to contend with the ecological challenges of foraging for food, to deal with increasing social complexity, and also to develop a more advanced brain.

▶ Ecological demands

Intelligence is perceived as being able to thrive in a given environment, especially by having foraging abilities. Humans adapted to global cooling in Paleolithic times by finding food and exploiting new environments due to the development of higher mental skills, such as cooperative hunting and tool use. Being a good forager required intelligence, which would incur a survival value.

▶ Foraging hypotheses

Milton (1988) hypothesised that increased intellect is due to the demands of foraging. Developing mental maps helped fruit-eaters to know when and where to look for food and they developed this ability by monitoring the availability of different fruits.

Gibson (1987) proposed the *food extraction hypothesis*, seeing the need to find hidden foods as having driven the evolution of intelligence. Cognitive processing, manual dexterity and tool use were necessary, creating selective pressure for a larger cortex.

Dunbar (1992) found no relationship between the amount of fruit in an animal's diet and the size of its neocortex. However, only small amounts of fruit may be needed for necessary nutrition.

Boesche et al. (1992) found that chimpanzees' use of tools to open nuts closely matched archaeological evidence of early nomadic humans noted for foraging skills, supporting Gibson's hypothesis.

- Milton's foraging hypothesis does not explain why fruit-eaters need a high-quality diet. Did they need more energy to fuel a larger brain, or did their brains grow to develop the skills to find fruit?
- Many animal species have maps for stored food items; therefore it seems unlikely that developing mental maps produces cognitive evolution.
- The food extraction hypothesis is difficult to test, as the level of difficulty in extracting foodstuffs is not well explained.

Social complexity hypothesis

Social living has advantages, but conflicts arise. Intelligent individuals are ones who can solve such problems. Intelligence is seen as social in nature and developing due to the need to anticipate, respond to and manipulate group members. There is a need to understand the mental world of others and to have Machiavellian intelligence to interact with and manipulate others. Advanced abilities in social cognition should be evident in those living in large, complex groups, and such animals should possess a large frontal cortex.

Holekamp and Engh (2003) found a relationship between brain size and complexity of social living in carnivores, supporting the hypothesis.

Ehmer et al. (2001) found larger brain structures in female paper wasps living in social colonies than in solitary females, supporting the hypothesis.

- Evidence from observations of animals often involves subjective interpretation that may be subject to researcher bias.
- An important ethical issue concerns taking care when performing studies on wild animals, not to lower their fitness in any way.

Brain size

The evolution of increased brain size is associated with the need for body coordination and to cope with the demands of group living, Machiavellian intelligence and ecological demands.

The *encephalisation quotient* comprises brain mass of a species divided by expected brain size for body size. Humans score highest, although some species outscore seemingly more intelligent ones. Humans possess the largest number of cortical neurons, although not enough to explain cognitive differences with other species.

The best measure of brain capacity is regarded as the number of cortical neurons combined with the conductive speed of cortical fibres, reflecting the speed of information processing. Humans are dominant.

Willerman et al. (1991) performed a meta-analysis of the relationship between brain volume and IQ, finding a positive correlation, suggesting that brain size and intelligence are related.

Sassaman and Zartler (1982) studied children with abnormally small brains: 40% were not retarded, suggesting that brain size may not reflect intelligence.

- Studies using IQ scores may be flawed as IQ only measures one aspect of intelligence.
- Humphrey (1999) believes that if big brains are not related to general intelligence, they must contribute to other evolutionary specialisms such as language abilities.

Q Outline and evaluate the role of evolutionary factors in the development of human intelligence. *(25 marks)*

2 *The role of genetic and environmental factors in intelligence test performance*

IQ tests claim to measure intelligence. Twin and adoption studies are conducted because if differences in IQ are genetic, people with close genetic relationships should have similar IQs. Also IQ levels should not be affected by experience, and attempts to increase IQ by enrichment should not work. Attempts have also been made to identify specific genes. Research findings have not drawn clear conclusions and attract controversy. The effect of cultural influences on IQ has proven divisive, especially attempts to create culture-free tests.

Genetic factors

Twin studies. These examine the relationship between people's genetic similarity and IQ scores. If the correlation is high, it is taken as evidence supporting the genetic argument.

> **Bouchard and McGue (1981)** found that identical twins had a much higher concordance rate than less related individuals. However, identical twins raised together often have identical environments.

- If intelligence were entirely genetic then concordance rates for identical twins would be 100%. As they are not, environment must play a role.

Adoption studies. If intelligence is genetic, adopted children should have IQ scores closer to those of their biological parents than of their adopted ones.

> **Petrill and Deater-Deckard (2004)** found that mothers were closer in IQ terms to biological than adopted children. However, IQ performance was related to age when adopted and time spent in the adoptive home, suggesting that environment also plays a role.

- Important factors are often not controlled and IQ scores of biological parents are difficult to confirm.
- Just like twin studies, adoption studies do not allow clear conclusions to be drawn.

Gene identification. Attempts have been made to identify specific genes involved in the inheritance of intelligence. Individual genes may only have slight influences, but collectively exert great influence.

> **Lahn et al. (2004)** identified a gene, ASPM, linked to higher intelligence. ASPM appears to affect the expansion of the cerebral cortex, which may explain how genes influence intelligence.

- Gene identification could help to understand not only intelligence but also learning disabilities and intellectual decay, leading to effective therapies.

Environmental factors

Family influences. IQ may be affected by how much social stimulation occurs.

> **Zajonc and Markus (1975)** found that as families grow in size, less stimulation is given to later children and their IQ is lower. However, the effect was small.

- Research implies that the fall in American IQ levels may be due to the trend for larger families and the reduced social stimulation that then occurs.

Enrichment. If intelligence is genetic then enrichment should not increase IQ.

Atkinson (1990) reviewed several enrichment programmes, finding that parental involvement, leading to stimulation at home, raised IQ levels and social skills.

- Parental involvement appears to be a key factor in boosting children's confidence and motivation to do well.
- In general, enrichment programmes seem able to boost intellectual performance, especially in the short term.

The influence of culture

IQ tests are biased in favour of the culture they represent, testing the skills and knowledge of that culture. Attempts have been made to create *culture-free tests* where questions are not culturally based and allow fair comparison of people. Poverty is a cultural factor, with minority cultural groups often living in impoverished conditions, which can have an effect on IQ levels.

Williams (1972) devised the Black Intelligence Test for Cultural Homogeneity (BITCH) based on black culture. Black people, who score poorly on traditional white-cultural tests, did well, while white people scored poorly, suggesting that IQ tests are culturally biased.

- Culture-free tests are culturally biased, as testing itself is a cultural concept.
- Vernon (1969) believes that intelligence is different things in different cultures and not something we all share in differing amounts measurable by IQ tests.

Q **(a)** Outline the role of environmental factors associated with intelligent test performance. *(5 marks)*

(b) Outline and evaluate the role of genetic factors associated with intelligent test performance. *(20 marks)*

8 Cognition and development

A Development of thinking

1 Theories of cognitive development

Theories of cognitive development attempt to explain the growth of mental abilities. Some theories see thought processes as undergoing qualitative changes as children age, with biological processes directing these changes. Other theorists believe that learning experiences are the major influence, with the relative influence of innate and environmental factors being a key issue.

Piaget

Piaget produced a theory of biological maturation seeing *qualitative* differences between adult and child thinking, with a set sequence of developmental stages and children only progressing when biologically ready.

An infant has basic reflexes and innate *schema* (ways of understanding the world). If new experiences fit the existing schema, they are *assimilated*. If they do not, they create *disequilibrium* (an unpleasant state of imbalance) and *accommodation* occurs where the existing schema change to fit in new experiences.

Assimilation and accommodation are *invariant processes* (remain the same).

Schemas and operations (internally consistent, logical mental rules) are *variant structures* (change as an individual develops).

A desire for *equilibrium* (pleasant state of balance) drives the process of development, new experiences pushing children into disequilibrium.

Stage of development	Description
Sensorimotor stage (0–2 years)	New schemas arise from matching sensory to motor experiences. Objective permanence occurs.
Pre-operational stage (2–7 years)	Internal images, symbols and language develop. Child influenced by how things seem, not logic.
Concrete operational stage (7–11 years)	Development of conservation (use of logical rules), but only if situations are concrete, not abstract. Decline of egocentrism.
Formal operational stage (11+ years)	Abstract manipulation of ideas (concepts without physical presence). Not achieved by all.

Piaget (1954) found that 3–4 month-old babies do not look for items out of view, suggesting that they have no object permanence. Bower and Wishart (1972) disagree, stating that 1 month-old babies show surprise when items disappear.

Piaget and Inhelder (1956) suggested that children under 7 years of age were egocentric, as they chose the view they could see of a model of mountains, rather than the doll's view asked for.

- Cross-cultural evidence suggests that the sequence of development is invariant and universal (except formal operations), and that it is a biological process of maturation.
- Due to poor methodology, Piaget underestimated what children could do.
- Piaget's theory functioned as a starting point for subsequent theories and research.

Vygotsky

Vygotsky saw the input of cultural knowledge as central to development. Knowledge and thinking are socially constructed by children interacting with people from their culture.

Culture changes *elementary mental functions* (innate capacities, such as attention) into *higher mental functions*, such as comprehension of language. Therefore, culture teaches children what and how to think, and there are several ways in which culture can influence cognitive development.

The *zone of proximal development* (ZPD) is the distance between current and potential ability. Cultural influences and experts push children through the ZPD and on to tasks beyond their current ability.

Scaffolding involves being given clues rather than answers. Learning first involves shared social activities, but eventually individuals self-scaffold and learning becomes an individual, self-regulated activity.

Semiotics help cognitive development through the use of language and other cultural symbols. These act as a medium for knowledge to be transmitted, turning elementary mental functions into higher ones.

First, children use *pre-intellectual language* for social and emotional purposes and *pre-linguistic thinking* occurs without language. From 2 years of age, language and thought combine.
- *Social speech* (0–3 years) — pre-intellectual language.
- *Egocentric speech* (3–7 years) — self-talk/thinking aloud.
- *Inner speech* (7 + years) — self-talk becomes silent and internal, and language is used for social communications.

From research Vygotsky proposed four stages of *concept formation*.

Stages of concept formation	Description
Vague syncretic	Trial and error formation without comprehension. Similar to Piaget's pre-operational stage.
Complex	Use of some strategies, but not very systematic.
Potential concept	More systematic with one attribute being focused on at a time (e.g. weight).
Mature concept	Several attributes can be dealt with systematically (e.g. weight and colour). Similar to Piaget's formal operations.

Berk (1994) found that children talked to themselves more when doing difficult tasks, supporting the idea of egocentric speech.

Wertsch et al. (1980) found that the amount of time children under 5 years of age spent looking at their mothers when assembling jigsaws decreased with age, supporting the idea of increased self-regulation.

- There is a lack of research support for the theory, but as it focuses on processes rather than outcomes, it is harder to test.
- The theory is more suited to collectivist cultures with more stress on social learning.

Bruner

Bruner was interested in the mental representation of knowledge, believing that children have an innate biological organisation aiding their understanding of the world. This develops in increasingly complex ways allowing more complex thinking, with learning occurring accidentally as children interact with their world. Learning occurs by organising information into categories, further organised into hierarchies, with the more general at the top.

Bruner proposed three *modes of representation* (different ways of cognitively representing the world).

Mode of representation	Description
Enactive (early childhood)	Knowledge is based on actions (muscle memories). Similar to sensorimotor stage.
Iconic (middle childhood)	Images of things and events experienced are built up.
Symbolic (adolescence)	Development of mental symbols (language) and logical thought.

The transition from *iconic* to *symbolic* mode at around 6 or 7 years of age is crucial. Bruner sees cognitive development as dependent on language development and a child's level of thinking as determined by its level of language.

Bruner and Kenney (1966) found that most 5 and 7 year-olds could memorise a matrix of nine glasses and reproduce them (iconic mode). When asked to transpose the glasses (give a reverse image of the glasses), no 5 year-olds, but 79% of 7 year-olds could do it (symbolic mode), suggesting that only older children could think using images and language.

- Bruner's theory stresses the role of biology and experience, language and social factors.
- Bruner agreed with Vygotsky that tutoring could develop potential.

Q Outline one theory of cognitive development. *(5 marks)*

2 *Applications of cognitive development to education*

All three theories have educational applications and research has assessed their effectiveness in actual classroom environments.

Piaget

Concept of readiness. A child is not capable of learning until ready, limiting what can be learned at a certain time. Teachers should teach age-related material in the order of development.

Discovery learning. Learning is child-centred, the child interacting with its environment and constructing knowledge itself. The teacher creates disequilibrium, making children accommodate new experiences and develop schemas.

Role of the teacher. Children's stages of development are assessed and suitable tasks are given to challenge them, creating disequilibrium. Relevant materials are provided at different ages. Opportunities for group learning are given as learning occurs from conflicting views, and peer interactions have social as well as cognitive value.

Modgil et al. (1983) found that discovery learning leads to poor reading and writing skills in children who need assistance.

Danner and Day (1977) found that coaching 10 and 13 year-olds had no effect, supporting Piaget's concept of readiness. However, it did assist 17 year-olds, suggesting that tuition helps at a later stage of development.

- Piaget never intended his theory as an educational tool; it was others who put it to this use.
- Walkerdine (1984) believes that educationalists used Piaget's theory as a convenient vehicle to justify changes they wished to make.

Vygotsky

Cooperative and collaborative thinking. Knowledge is socially constructed by learners working collectively on a common task. Individuals depend upon and are accountable to each other, helping individuals to work better on their own.

Peer tutoring. Allowing peers to be tutors creates a beneficial learning experience for the tutor.

Expert tutoring. This is an effective teaching tool if the boundaries of a child's ZPD are taken into account.

Scaffolding. Experienced people assist development, providing general and specific tutoring, and enabling individuals to achieve. Eventually, scaffolding becomes self-instruction.

Cloward (1967) found peer tutoring more beneficial for the tutor than the designated learner, demonstrating the benefit of the method.

Gokhale (1995) tested students on critical thinking, finding that those undertaking collaborative learning outscored those studying alone, supporting the idea of cooperative learning.

- Learning via cooperative groups needs monitoring or some individuals dominate and others coast.
- Vygotsky's approach works less well in individualistic settings, with emphasis on competitiveness and autonomy.

Bruner

Discovery learning. Emphasis is on the active role of the learner, teachers having a central role, offering direct tuition and providing strategies for self-learning, and identifying specific cognitive abilities required for a task and any consistent errors that learners make. Pupils organise information themselves, integrating it into existing hierarchical structures or adapting it into new hierarchies. Learning involves accumulating information and creating structure for the information.

Scaffolding. Adult and peer tutors give tuition, enabling pupils to achieve.

Spiral curriculum. Concepts are mastered by revisiting them at different ages, redeveloping them with increased complexity when more mature modes of thought permit.

Materials and activities. Children are provided with study materials, activities and tools matching and cultivating cognitive abilities. There is a transition as children progress through different modes of thought, from using concrete, to pictorial and then symbolic activities, creating more effective learning. Using appropriate, stimulating materials and activities creates motivation for learning to occur.

Leat (1998) found Bruner's methods incorporated successfully into the teaching of geography.

Smith (2002) reported that Bruner's idea of intuitive and analytical thinking was successfully introduced into schools.

- The idea of a spiral curriculum has met with a lot of praise, as well as Bruner's idea of structured learning.
- Bruner's work greatly influenced Gardner's construction of his theory of multiple intelligences.

Q (a) Outline one theory of cognitive development *(9 marks)*
(b) Evaluate the theory outlined in (a) in terms of its application to education *(16 marks)*

B Development of moral understanding

1 Kohlberg's theory of moral understanding

Kohlberg (1966) sees morality as developing in innate stages in a set order. Morality develops when biological maturation is ready, with disequilibrium playing a part, as experiences not fitting existing schemas challenge current ways of thinking about morality. Women are seen as less morally developed, as they are restricted to a domestic life.

Each stage of morality involves a different kind of thinking to reach moral decisions, the focus being on how moral thinking occurs, rather than on what is thought about a moral issue. Moral behaviour is seen as a result of moral thinking.

Kohlberg created his theory from ten moral dilemmas with no 'right' or 'wrong' answers, which he gave to participants. One dilemma involved a chemist who will not give Heinz a drug that will save his dying wife, because he cannot immediately afford it. The moral dilemma is whether Heinz is right to steal the drug. Kohlberg is not interested in whether participants think it is right to steal, but on the reasoning behind their answer. From this he created three levels of morality, each one containing two stages.

Level of morality	Description
1 Pre-conventional (age 6–13)	Stage one: morality based on outcomes (e.g. punishments), rather than intentions. Stage two: moral rules followed when it benefits us.
2 Conventional (age 13–16)	Stage three: morality based on 'being good' and maintaining trust and loyalty of others. Stage four: morality based on what is best for society, fulfilling our duty.
3 Post-conventional (age 16–20)	Stage five: social order seen as paramount, with realisation that bad rules can be changed. Stage six: adherence to a personal set of moral rules.

Kohlberg (1969) tested the moral reasoning of participants in several cultures, finding the same sequence of moral development. This suggests that transition through the stages occurs as an innate biological process.

Kohlberg (1975) tested whether moral reasoning reflects moral behaviour. He gave students a chance to cheat on a test and found that 15% of those with post-conventional morality cheated, while 70% of those with pre-conventional morality did, supporting the prediction.

Berkowitz and Gibbs (1983) found that development through the stages was assisted by transactive interactions, where discussions are held about moral possibilities. This supports Kohlberg's idea that creating disequilibrium in an individual's way of thinking develops moral growth.

Fodor (1972) compared delinquents' and non-delinquents' levels of morality, finding non-delinquents at a higher level, supporting the notion that moral thinking reflects actual moral behaviour.

- As only 12% of adults reach post-conventional morality, Atkinson et al. (1990) argued that it is more of a philosophical ideal than part of a normal developmental sequence.
- Moral dilemmas are not real-life scenarios; people may behave quite differently from their moral reasoning if actually placed in such situations. Gilligan (1982) questioned women deciding whether to have abortions and found different patterns of moral thought from Kohlberg, although this may be due to using females rather than males.

- Kohlberg's theory is accused of gender bias. He saw morality based on principles of justice, while Gilligan argues that women operate on principles of care. Kohlberg's negative rating of female morality may be a result of being assessed by male-created standards and methodological faults, such as using only male participants.

Q Outline and evaluate Kohlberg's theory of moral understanding. *(25 marks)*

2 *Eisenberg's theory of pro-social reasoning*

Eisenberg's (1986) theory includes the element of emotion not present in Kohlberg's theory and centres on the idea of giving help and comfort to others. Similar to Kohlberg, Eisenberg sees moral development occurring along with the development of general cognitive abilities.

A key feature is the idea of empathy, seeing from another's viewpoint, so the emotions of others can be appreciated. Therefore Eisenberg emphasised role-taking skills, involving consideration of another person's perspective.

Similar to Kohlberg, Eisenberg used moral dilemmas, but involving conflict between one's own needs and those of others, with the influence of laws, rules, obligations, possible punishments, etc. at a minimum, and with an option to bring help and comfort to others, but at a personal cost. Younger children make decisions in a self-centred manner, while older children take others' feelings into consideration. Again like Kohlberg, she used findings from her own research to propose a theory of five levels.

Level of pro-social reasoning	Description
1 Hedonistic (pre-school/early primary school)	Pro-social behaviour occurs when it benefits self.
2 Needs oriented (a few pre-school/mainly primary school)	Some consideration of others. Little evidence of sympathy or guilt for self-centredness.
3 Approval oriented (primary school/a few early secondary school)	Pro-social behaviour evident when it elicits praise from others.
4 Empathetic (late primary school/secondary school)	Some evidence of sympathy and guilt. Some reference to moral principles and obligations.
5 Strongly internalised (a few primary school/some secondary school)	Evidence of internalised principles important to self-respect.

Eisenberg (1986) found evidence from studies of European samples of her levels of pro-social reasoning being cross-cultural, suggesting a link to biological maturation. However, evidence from collectivist cultures, such as kibbutz communes in Israel, indicates a lack of needs orientation, with reasoning more directed by communally based beliefs, suggesting that her theory does not fit non-Western cultures.

Caplan and Hay (1989) found that 3 to 5 year-olds demonstrated distress at another child's distress, but seldom attempt assistance, supporting the idea that empathy needs to be experienced for pro-social behaviour to occur.

Chalmers and Townsend (1990) found that girls with poor social skills were able to develop empathy and concern for others, if they received coaching in role-taking skills, suggesting that empathy can be learned and the use of role taking can facilitate this process.

Feshbach (1982) found evidence of females being more empathetic than males, while **Aries and Johnson (1983)** found females more likely to offer emotional support. However, **Eisenberg (1986)** reports that boys develop more slowly and become empathetic during adolescence.

- The theory has practical applications, such as the training of parents and others involved in child-care, in how to encourage and develop empathy in children, such as getting them to look after pets, or share toys.
- Although Eisenberg's theory is broader than Kohlberg's, incorporating the important element of emotion, there are many similarities, so it can be considered a development of Kohlberg's theory, rather than a separate theory.
- The methodology used in Eisenberg's research is more valid than Kohlberg's, as her moral dilemmas were more suited to use with young children.
- It is possible that the development of empathy occurs earlier than Eisenberg stated. Zahn-Waxler et al. (1979) found concern for distressed others in children as young as 18 months.

Q Critically compare one theory of moral understanding and one theory of pro-social reasoning. *(25 marks)*

C Development of social cognition

1 Development of the child's sense of self

Self-recognition. Having a sense of 'self' is an important factor in social interaction and is associated with types of intelligence required for social living.

Self-recognition is assessed by the *mirror test*, where a coloured mark is made on the face and the participant placed in front of a mirror. If the participant touches the mark, they are perceived as being able to self-recognise. Some can do this at 15 months and the majority by 2 years of age. The idea is that, for an individual to comprehend whom the mirror image is of, there must be a mental representation of self.

Mans et al. (1978) showed that self-recognition in Down's syndrome children was delayed, but by 4 years of age 89% could do it, suggesting that recognition of self, and thus self-awareness, is related to cognitive development.

Gender concept. Most children develop *gender identity*, where they realise if they are male or female, between 2 and 3 years of age. Between 3 and 7 years, *gender stability* develops, where it is realised that gender is fixed, and by 12 years of age, *gender consistency* is achieved, where it is realised that changes in appearance or activity do not alter one's gender.

The distinction between the physical and the psychological self. The ability to differentiate between physical and psychological self demonstrates awareness of a private, unseen self. Children between 3 and 4 years of age are aware of the distinction, but mainly refer to themselves in physical terms.

Selman (1980) believed that children under the age of 6 could not distinguish between physical and psychological selves. By the age of 8, most children had developed the ability.

Self-referential emotions. Certain emotions, such as embarrassment, convey a sense of self-awareness, involving thinking about yourself in relation to others.

Lewis et al. (1989) found that when children are asked to dance in front of adults, they display embarrassment around the same age that they demonstrate self-recognition.

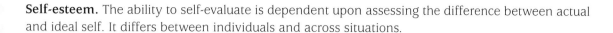

Self-esteem. The ability to self-evaluate is dependent upon assessing the difference between actual and ideal self. It differs between individuals and across situations.

> **Vershueren et al. (2001)** found that children between 4 and 5 years of age have a sense of self-esteem and it is related to attachment patterns, with securely attached individuals having higher levels.

Theory of Mind (ToM). Comprehension of another's thoughts and emotions is perceived as indicating intelligence. It is assessed with the Sally-Anne test, which looks for realisation of false beliefs. ToM seems to develop around 4 years of age, with the amygdala and basal ganglia especially associated with ToM processing. With ToM development comes the ability to manipulate and deceive by hiding emotions and intentions.

> **Avis and Harris (1991)** found that children in developed and non-developed countries realise at 4 years of age that people can have false beliefs, supporting the idea of biological maturation.

- A methodological difficulty in researching the development of social cognition is the lack of language skills in small children, making it difficult to arrive at conclusions.

Q Describe and evaluate the development of the child's sense of self. *(25 marks)*

2 Development of children's understanding of others

With the development of a sense of self comes the ability to understand others. The ability to self-recognise occurs simultaneously to acquiring empathy, at around 18 months of age.

Perspective taking

Perspective taking concerns the ability to assume another's perspective and understand their thoughts and feelings. Selman (1980) proposed *role-taking theory*, where adopting the perspective of another allows comprehension of their feelings, thoughts and intentions. The theory has five levels and was developed through using *interpersonal dilemmas*, such as whether expert tree-climber Holly, who promised her father she will not climb trees, should climb a tree to save a kitten.

As children mature, they take more information into account, coming to realise that people can react differently to the same situation. They develop the ability to analyse people's perspectives from the viewpoint of an objective, neutral bystander and have a realisation of how different cultural and societal values affect the perception of the bystander.

Stage of perspective taking	Description
Undifferentiated (age 3–6)	Recognises that self and others have different thoughts and feelings, but often confuse the two.
Social informational (age 5–9 years)	Recognises that different perspectives arise, as people have access to different information.
Self-reflective (age 7–12 years)	Can perceive others' feelings, thoughts and behaviour from their perspective.
Third party (age 10–15)	Can step outside a two-person situation, viewing it from a third-party, neutral viewpoint.
Societal (14–adult)	Understands that third-party perspectives can be influenced by societal value systems.

Selman's stages of perspective taking

Schultz and Selman (1990) found that the transition from self-centred perspectives to an ability to perceive from others' perspectives is related to the development of enhanced interpersonal negotiation skills and concern for others, suggesting that perspective taking plays a key role in social maturation.

Underwood and Moore (1982) found the ability to perspective take positively correlated with prosocial behaviour, suggesting that perspective taking enhances social relationships.

- The theory has practical applications as a means of conflict resolution. Walker and Selman (1998) used perspective taking to reduce violence levels by getting individuals to empathise with other people's feelings and viewpoints.
- A lot of research into perspective taking is correlational and so does not show causality. Other mediating factors may be involved.
- Selman's stage theory and use of dilemmas provides researchers with an objective means of assessing social competence.

Q   Outline the development of children's understanding of others.   *(9 marks)*

3   *Biological explanations of social cognition*

It is thought that biological factors, such as genes and brain processes, interact with environmental variables, producing individual differences in social competence. Social interactive success is dependent upon the development of brain systems geared to processing social information. Although learning experiences are necessary for normal development, without innate neural systems processing social stimuli, it is difficult to explain the universality and speed of social learning. Brain abnormalities impair social interactions, suggesting that social skills are directed by brain systems. Brain imaging studies indicate that a network of brain areas linking the medial prefrontal and temporal cortex form the neural substrate of mentalising, allowing representation of your own and others' mental states.

Mirror neurons. These are nerves in the brain, active when a specific action is performed or observed in others, allowing the observer to experience the action as if it were theirs, and permitting us to sample the feelings and thoughts of others by empathising with and imitating them, and to have a ToM.

Rizzolato and Craighero (2004) used brain scanning to find a network of neurons in the frontal and parietal brain areas appearing to work as mirror neurons.

Gallese (2001) used fMRI scanning to find the anterior cingulate cortex and inferior frontal cortex, active when an individual experiences emotion or observes another experiencing the same emotion, suggesting mirror neuron type activity.

Stuss et al. (2001) reported that individuals with damage to their frontal lobes often had an inability to empathise with and read other people's intentions and were easy to deceive, suggesting a biological link to social cognition.

- There is a methodological problem in studying mirror neurons in humans: it is not possible to study the actions of single neurons.
- Social cognition seems to only exist in some higher animals, suggesting that it has a biological basis, which has evolved due to its adaptive advantage.
- Jacob and Jeannerod (2004) point out that a mirror neuron system is too simplistic, as it cannot explain how the same actions performed in others can be interpreted differently by an observer in different contexts.

Q   **(a)** Outline the role of the mirror neuron system.   *(9 marks)*
      (b) Evaluate biological explanations of social cognition.   *(16 marks)*

Unit 4

Psychopathology, psychology in action and research methods

9 Psychopathology

A Schizophrenia

1 Clinical characteristics

Schizophrenia affects thought processes and ability to determine reality. It is the world's most common mental disorder, 1% of people suffering from the condition.

Degree of severity varies, some only encountering one episode, some having persistent episodes, but living relatively normal lives through taking medication, while others have episodes unresponsive to medication, remaining disturbed.

Type I is an acute type characterised by positive symptoms, such as thought disorders, and Type II is a chronic type characterised by negative symptoms, such as apathy, and with a poorer prospect for recovery.

Diagnosis requires two or more symptoms to be apparent for more than 1 month, as well as reduced social functioning.

Symptoms can be *positive*, where distortion of normal functioning occurs, or *negative*, where there is a lessening of normal functioning. *Chronic onset schizophrenia* occurs where a person gradually withdraws and loses motivation over time. *Acute onset schizophrenia* occurs where symptoms appear suddenly after a stressful incident.

Schizophrenia commonly occurs between 15 and 45 years of age, with an equal incidence of males and females, though males show onset at an earlier age.

Symptoms

Passivity experiences and thought disorders. Thoughts and actions are perceived as under external control (e.g. by aliens etc.) Sufferers may believe that thoughts are being inserted, withdrawn or broadcast to others

Auditory hallucinations. Sufferers experience internal voices, which form a running commentary, or appear to discuss the sufferer's behaviour.

Primary delusions. Sufferers may experience *delusions of grandeur*, thinking they are someone important, such as Jesus Christ. Later, delusions may become *delusions of persecution*, sufferers believing that someone is 'out to get them'.

Thought-process disorders. Sufferers wander off the point, or their words become muddled, or new words and phrases are invented.

Disturbances of effect. Sufferers appear indifferent, or exhibit inappropriate emotional responses, or display mood changes.

Psychomotor disturbances. Sufferers exhibit 'statue'-like poses, tics and twitches, or repetitive behaviours.

Lack of volition. Sufferers display an inability to make decisions, have no enthusiasm and do not display affection.

Sub-types

Paranoid. This is characterised by delusions of grandeur and/or persecution with less noticeable disturbance than other types.

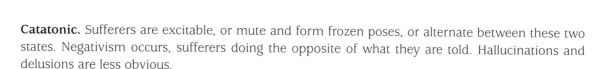

Catatonic. Sufferers are excitable, or mute and form frozen poses, or alternate between these two states. Negativism occurs, sufferers doing the opposite of what they are told. Hallucinations and delusions are less obvious.

Disorganised (Hebephrenic). Onset occurs in the early to mid-twenties, sufferers experiencing auditory hallucinations, delusions, thought-process disorders and disturbances of effect. Behaviour can appear bizarre.

Residual. Sufferers exhibited symptoms previously, but not presently, negative symptoms having been experienced during the past year. Sufferers display mild positive symptoms.

Undifferentiated. This is a category for schizophrenics who do not fit any other types, or who have symptoms of several sub-types.

Simple. This appears in late adolescence with a gradual onset. There is an increase in apathy and social deterioration, with a decline in academic or occupational performance.

Post-schizophrenic depression. This is a sub-type for schizophrenics meeting criteria for the disorder in the last year, though not at present, exhibiting severe and prolonged depressive symptoms.

Q Outline clinical characteristics of schizophrenia. *(5 marks)*

2 *Issues surrounding classification and diagnosis*

Reliability

Reliability refers to the consistency of measurements and affects classification and diagnosis.
- *Test–retest reliability* occurs when a practitioner makes consistent diagnoses on separate occasions from the same information.
- *Inter-rater reliability* occurs when several practitioners make identical, independent diagnoses of the same patient.

Beck et al. (1962) reported a 54% concordance rate between experienced practitioners' diagnoses, while **Söderberg et al. (2005)** reported a concordance rate of 81% using DSM-IV-TR, the most up-to-date form of the DSM (Diagnostic and Statistical Manual) classification system, suggesting that classification systems have become more reliable over time.

Read et al. (2004) reports test–retest reliability of schizophrenia diagnosis to have only a 37% concordance rate.

- The DSM classification system (used in the UK) is seen as more reliable than the ICD (International Classification of Disorders) because of the amount of specificity in the symptoms outlined for each category.
- Even if reliability of diagnosis based on classification systems is poor, it allows practitioners to have a common language, permitting communication of research ideas and findings, which may lead to a better understanding of the disorder and effective treatments.
- Evidence suggests that reliability of diagnoses has improved as classification systems have been updated.

Validity

Validity concerns how accurate, meaningful and useful diagnosis is. There are a number of ways in which validity can be assessed. For instance:

Reliability. A valid diagnosis has first to be reliable (though reliability is no guarantee of validity).

Predictive validity. If diagnosis leads to successful treatment, the diagnosis can be seen as valid.

Descriptive validity. For diagnosis to be valid, patients diagnosed with different disorders should actually differ from each other.

Aetiological validity. For diagnosis to be valid, patients diagnosed as schizophrenic should have the same cause for their disorder.

Hollis (2000) applied DSM classification diagnoses to case notes, finding that the diagnosis of schizophrenia had a high level of stability. This suggests diagnoses to be valid.

Heather (1976) reported that few causes of mental disorders are known and that there is only a 50% chance of predicting what treatment a patient will receive based on diagnosis, suggesting that diagnosis is not valid.

Jansson and Parnas (2007) reviewed studies that applied different definitions of schizophrenia to the same patient samples. Both ICD-10 and DSM-IV showed reliability, but both were weak on measures of validity, casting doubt on whether schizophrenia exists as a separate condition.

- Bentall (2003) says that the diagnosis of schizophrenia reveals nothing about the causes, implying diagnosis to be invalid. Diagnosis also reveals nothing about prevalence rates, which differ widely from rural to urban environments, again suggesting diagnosis to be invalid.
- Cochrane (1977) reported that the incidence of schizophrenia in the West Indies and the UK is 1%, but that people of Afro-Caribbean origin are seven times more likely to be diagnosed as schizophrenic when living in the UK, suggesting that Afro-Caribbean people living in the UK either have more stressors leading to schizophrenia, or are receiving invalid diagnoses due to cultural bias.

Q To what extent are diagnoses of schizophrenia reliable? *(25 marks)*

3 Biological explanations

Evidence from biological explanations, focused on genetics, evolution, biochemistry, neuroanatomy and pregnancy factors, suggests that biological factors play a major contributory role.

Genetics. Findings from twin, family, adoption and gene mapping studies suggest a genetic component, making some individuals more vulnerable.

Torrey et al. (1994) found that if one identical twin develops schizophrenia, there is a 28% chance that the other twin will too.

Kety and Ingraham (1992) found schizophrenia to be ten times higher among genetic than adoptive relatives, suggesting that genetics play a greater role.

Varma and Sharma (1993) found a concordance rate of 35% for first-degree relatives of schizophrenics, but only 9% in first-degree relatives of non-schizophrenics, indicating a genetic factor

Benzel et al. (2007) used gene mapping to find that an interaction of genetic factors creates a susceptibility to schizophrenia.

- Hedgecoe (2001) believes scientists construct schizophrenia as a genetic disease by using evidence in a biased way to produce a narrative about schizophrenia, prioritising genetic explanations.
- Varma and Sharma (1993) believe that family studies can identify samples for further research that have an increased probability of carrying the schizophrenic genotype.

Evolutionary explanations. These suggest an adaptive value to schizophrenia. Stevens and Price (1997) propose the *group-splitting hypothesis*, where those possessing schizophrenic qualities make ideal leaders when groups split due to environmental pressures.

Biological explanations

Peters et al. (1999) studied religious cults, finding leaders to be charismatic and possessing delusional beliefs, supporting the group-splitting hypothesis.

Storr (1997) cites examples of group leaders possessing schizotypal, paranoid, psychopathic qualities, such as David Koresh and Adolf Hitler.

- Although some leaders possess schizophrenic like qualities, the majority of leaders do not, even in new, breakaway social groupings, weakening support for the theory.

Biochemical explanations. These centre on the idea that excess dopamine leads to the onset of schizophrenia and, indeed, that many anti-schizophrenic drugs inhibit dopamine activity. Davis et al. (1991) suggest that high levels of dopamine in the mesolimbic dopamine system are associated with positive symptoms, while high levels in the mesocortical dopamine system are associated with negative symptoms. The neurotransmitter glutamate also attracts attention, due to reduced function of NMDA glutamate receptors in schizophrenics.

Iversen (1979) reported that dead schizophrenics have an excess of dopamine in their limbic systems, supporting the explanation.

Javitt et al. (2000) found that glycine, a glutamate receptor agonist, reduced schizophrenic symptoms, supporting the glutamate theory.

- Healy (2000) believes that pharmaceutical companies were keen to see the dopamine theory promoted, as they had made profits from manufacturing anti-schizophrenic drugs that inhibited dopamine production.
- Excess dopamine could be an effect rather than a cause of schizophrenia.

Neuroanatomical explanations. Enlarged ventricles are found in the brains of some dead schizophrenics and MRI scans have located structural abnormalities in many sufferers, especially those with Type II schizophrenia, although such abnormalities may be the result of being disturbed for many years rather than a causal factor.

Torrey (2002) reported enlarged ventricles in schizophrenics, which may result from reduced development in certain brain areas.

Kim et al. (2000) used MRI scans to find that some schizophrenics have small frontal lobes and abnormal blood flow in certain brain areas, supporting the explanation.

- Dean (1999) reported that using neuropletics to treat schizophrenia leads to structural abnormalities, which therefore are not causal factors.
- MRI scans suggest that schizophrenia is associated with structural abnormalities, but different studies cannot agree which brain areas are affected.

Pregnancy. Many schizophrenics are born in the winter, and as many viral infections occur during wintertime, interest has focused on whether infections contracted during pregnancy make unborn children more vulnerable to developing the disorder. Indeed, structural and biochemical abnormalities associated with schizophrenia may actually occur from damage during pregnancy.

Torrey et al. (1988) reported that surges of schizophrenic cases correspond to flu pandemics, supporting the idea of viral infections in pregnancy being a causal factor.

Khashan et al. (2008) found that children born to mothers with stress in early pregnancy had an increased risk of developing schizophrenia, supporting the explanation.

TOPIC 9 Psychopathology

- Not everyone experiencing pregnancy infections develops schizophrenia, implying that other factors must be involved.
- The risk is small, with 97% of babies born to women with flu while pregnant not developing the disorder.

Q (a) Outline two biological explanations of schizophrenia. *(9 marks)*
(b) Evaluate one of the biological explanations of schizophrenia outlined in (a). *(16 marks)*

4 Psychological explanations

Psychological explanations of schizophrenia include the behaviourist, cognitive, psychodynamic and sociocultural explanations. Although evidence indicates biological factors to be important, it is generally accepted that psychological factors are involved too.

Behaviourist explanations. Operant conditioning explains schizophrenia as being learned, with people reinforced for bizarre behaviour due to the attention it brings. Alternatively, escaping to an inner world may be rewarding as an escape from real-world pressures, leading to people being labelled as schizophrenic and then behaving in a way that meets the requirements of the label.

Liberman (1982) reported that children learn to be schizophrenic by being reinforced for bizarre responses to inappropriate stimuli and such reinforcements lead to even more bizarre behaviour and eventually psychosis.

- Behaviourism cannot explain why schizophrenics exhibit similar symptoms without having witnessed such behaviour before, or why the disorder tends to occur in late adolescence/early adulthood.

Psychodynamic explanations. These propose that schizophrenics have experienced either interpersonal regression or interpersonal withdrawal, with stress seen as a contributory factor and an emphasis on the personality characteristics of parents, the interactions between parents and children and family structures.

Read et al. (2005) reviewed studies of schizophrenia, finding a link between sexual abuse in childhood and later development of schizophrenia. In addition, schizophrenia was the most common mental disorder for victims of sexual abuse, supporting the psychodynamic explanation.

- There is little empirical data to back up the psychodynamic theory, most evidence coming from subjective analyses of case studies, which rely upon honesty and accuracy of recall during psychoanalysis.

Cognitive explanations. These see schizophrenia as linked to maladaptive thinking, and symptoms such as disorganised thinking suggest a cognitive input.

Frith (1992) suggests that positive symptoms of schizophrenia, such as delusions, are problems of metarepresentation where there is an inability to distinguish external speech from internal thoughts. Conversely, negative symptoms, such as disorganised thinking, are problems of central control, where there is a failure to distinguish between behaviour of conscious intent and that of automatic response.

Bentall et al. (1991) found that schizophrenics struggled to identify words belonging to a certain category (e.g. birds), which they had read earlier, had created themselves or had not seen before, supporting Frith's theory of schizophrenics having metarepresentation problems.

Biological therapies

- Kane and Lencz (2008) propose that the inclusion of cognitive impairment in the diagnostic criteria for schizophrenia would improve the validity of diagnosis and treatments by targeting cognitive enhancement as a primary goal.

Sociocultural explanations. The degree of *expressed emotion* within families (e.g. hostility) may be an indicator of relapse in schizophrenics, contributing to the disorder's maintenance.

The *double-bind theory* sees schizophrenia as a learned response to conflicting messages and mutually exclusive demands during childhood, leading to disorganised thinking and communication.

Social causation perceives the lower social classes as subject to more stressors, causing heightened levels of schizophrenia.

Leff (1976) reported a relapse rate of 51% for schizophrenics returning to homes with high expressed emotion compared to 13% for schizophrenics returning to homes with low rates of expressed emotion.

- Social-cultural factors may be effects rather than causes of schizophrenia. For example, expressed emotions may occur within families due to the stresses and conflicts associated with living with a schizophrenic, rather than contributing to the condition's onset.

Q Outline and evaluate psychological explanations of schizophrenia. *(25 marks)*

5 | *Biological therapies*

Electro-convulsive therapy

Cerletti (1935) believed that inducing an epileptic fit would remove schizophrenic symptoms from sufferers. Over time this was not deemed successful, but electro-convulsive therapy (ECT) has now been reintroduced and is seen as more effective than placebos, though not as effective as drug treatment. ECT works best when applied bilaterally (to both sides of the head). Treatments are given in conjunction with an anaesthetic and a muscle relaxant.

Tharyan and Adams (2005) reviewed studies of ECT, concluding that it is an effective treatment in the short term, being better than no treatment, but not as effective as anti-psychotic drugs.

Tang et al. (2002) found ECT effective in treating schizophrenics who did not respond positively to treatment with anti-psychotic drugs, suggesting that the treatment provides relief to such patients.

Fisk (1997) reported ECT to have a success rate of up to 80%, but that it is only effective against certain categories of schizophrenia and more treatments are needed than with other disorders.

- Up to 50% of schizophrenics who respond positively to ECT relapse within 6 months, suggesting that it does not offer a long-term solution
- Unilateral ECT treatment produces fewer side-effects, such as short-term memory loss, but is not as effective in treating the disorder. Memory generally returns to normal, but 1% suffer severe memory loss.
- ECT is no more dangerous than minor surgery under general anaesthetic, with a death rate of approximately 1 in 10,000.

Drugs

The prime treatment for schizophrenia is anti-psychotic drugs, which do not cure the condition, but dampen symptoms down so that a normal degree of functioning becomes possible.

Antipsychotics are divided into first- (typical) and second-generation (atypical) varieties. Typical varieties, such as chloropromazine, arrest dopamine production by blocking the receptors in synapses that absorb dopamine, thus reducing positive symptoms, such as auditory hallucinations.

Atypical antipsychotics, such as clozapine, work by acting upon serotonin as well as dopamine production systems and affect negative symptoms, such as reduced emotional expression.

Some sufferers only take a course of antipsychotics once, while others have to take a regular dose in order to prevent schizophrenic symptoms reappearing. There is a sizeable minority who do not respond to drug treatment.

Kahn et al. (2008) found that antipsychotics are generally effective for at least one year, but that second-generation drugs were no more effective than first-generation ones.

Davis et al. (1989) performed a meta-analysis of studies comparing antipsychotics with placebos, finding drugs more effective. Over 70% of sufferers treated with antipsychotics improving in condition after 6 weeks, while less than 25% improved with placebos, suggesting that antipsychotics have a beneficial effect.

- Antipsychotics are effective as they are relatively cheap to produce, easy to administer and have a positive effect on many sufferers, allowing them to live relatively normal lives outside mental institutions.
- One problem with antipsychotics is the high relapse rate, occurring through not taking medication on a regular basis, or even when doing so.
- Although antipsychotics can produce relatively minor side-effects, such as constipation, some sufferers incur serious neurological symptoms leading to coma and death.

Q Outline and evaluate one biological therapy for the treatment of schizophrenia. Refer to research evidence in your answer.

(20 marks)

6   *Psychological therapies*

Behavioural therapy

Although there is little evidence that schizophrenia is learned, success in treating it is attained through *token economies*, behavioural change being achieved by awarding tokens for desired actions. These reinforcers are exchanged for goods or privileges. The technique reduces negative symptoms such as poor motivation, and nurses subsequently view patients more positively, which has beneficial outcomes for patients.

McMonagle and Sultana (2000) reviewed token economy regimes over a 15-year period, finding that they did reduce negative symptoms, though it was unclear if behavioural changes were maintained beyond the treatment programme.

Upper and Newton (1971) found that the weight gain associated with taking antipsychotics was addressed with token economy regimes. Chronic schizophrenics achieved a target of 3lbs of body weight loss a week.

- Changes in behaviour achieved through token economies do not remain when tokens are withdrawn, suggesting that such treatments address effects of schizophrenia rather than causes.
- The focus of a token economy is on shaping and positively reinforcing desired behaviours, not on punishing undesirable behaviours.

Psychodynamic therapy

Psychodynamic treatments provide insight into the link between symptoms and early experiences. Poor early relationships create a poor sense of self, leading to schizophrenics having faulty metarepresentation and being unable to distinguish thoughts from external sources. The therapist provides a surrogate parenting role, facilitating normal personality development and allowing proper metarepresentation so that patients can distinguish their thoughts from those of others.

Malmberg and Fenton (2009) found that psychodynamic therapies have little benefit unless used with drug treatments, suggesting that only with the use of antipsychotics can patients benefit from talking therapies.

Knapp et al. (1994) found problem-orientated, home-based psychotherapy to be cost-effective, producing 'mildly encouraging' results and suggesting some support for psychotherapy.

- The use of psychodynamic therapies as a sole treatment for schizophrenia has rarely been evaluated, suggesting that it is difficult to draw conclusions about such treatments.
- Barton (1976) believes that psychotherapy has an advantage over other treatments as it can be administered outside hospitals, reducing the risk of institutionalisation.

Cognitive-behavioural therapy

Cognitive-behavioural therapy (CBT) is the main psychological treatment used with schizophrenia, although antipsychotics are also used to reduce psychotic thought processes.

The idea is that beliefs, expectations and cognitive assessments of self, the environment and the nature of personal problems affect how a person perceives themselves and others, how problems are approached and how successful a person is in coping and attaining goals. CBT identifies and alters irrational thinking. Drawings are employed to display the links between a sufferer's thoughts, actions and emotions, with comprehension of where symptoms come from being very useful in reducing a sufferer's anxiety levels.

Turkington et al. (2006) assessed practices and data concerning CBT as a treatment for schizophrenia, concluding that it is highly effective and should be used as a mainstream treatment wherever possible.

Tarrier (2005) reviewed trials of CBT, finding evidence of reduced symptoms, especially positive ones, and lower relapse rates.

- For CBT to be effective, training is essential, successful treatment being dependent upon developing empathy, respect, unconditional positive regard and honesty between patient and practitioner.
- CBT is not suitable for all patients, especially those who are too thought disorientated or agitated, who refuse medication, or who are too paranoid to form trusting alliances with practitioners.

Q **(a)** Outline the clinical characteristics of schizophrenia. *(5 marks)*
   (b) Describe and evaluate psychological therapies for schizophrenia. *(20 marks)*

B Depression

1 *Clinical characteristics*

Symptoms

Constant depressed mood — feelings of sadness, reported by the sufferer or observed by others.

Lessened interest — diminished concern with and/or lack of pleasure in daily activities, reported by sufferer or observed by others.

Weight loss — significant decrease (or increase) in weight and/or appetite.

Sleep pattern disturbance — constant insomnia or oversleeping .

Fatigue — loss of energy and displacement of energy levels: for example, becoming lethargic or agitated.

Reduced concentration — difficulty in paying attention, slowed thinking and/or indecisiveness, reported by the sufferer or observed by others.

Worthlessness — constant feelings of reduced worth and/or inappropriate guilt.

Focus on death — constant thoughts of death and/or suicide.

- At least five symptoms must be apparent every day for at least 2 weeks for depression to be diagnosed, with an impairment in general functioning evident that cannot be accounted for by other medical conditions. One of the five symptoms should either be a constant depressed mood or lessened interest in daily activities.

Sub-types

Unipolar. This is differentiated from bipolar depression by manifesting itself purely as depression without manic episodes.

Bipolar. This involves different types of episodes, including depressive ones, plus manic episodes where the sufferer is aroused and has trouble concentrating, while simultaneously displaying elevated self-esteem and an excessive involvement in pleasurable, but harmful activities, such as drug taking.

Q Outline clinical characteristics of depression. *(5 marks)*

2 Issues surrounding classification and diagnosis

Reliability

Reliability refers to the consistency of measurements and affects classification and diagnosis of depression in two ways:
- *Test–retest reliability* occurs when a practitioner makes consistent diagnoses on separate occasions from the same information.
- *Inter-rater reliability* occurs when several practitioners make identical, independent diagnoses of the same patient.

Moods vary over time in most people, so diagnosing depression reliably is difficult. Another problem is assessing the degree to which sufferers are depressed.

Diagnosis was originally performed by clinical interviews, but use is increasingly made of depression inventories.

Einfeld et al. (2002) found a high level of agreement between skilled clinicians in diagnosing depression, implying a high degree of inter-rater reliability.

Sato et al. (1996) assessed the test–retest reliability of the Inventory to Diagnose Depression, Lifetime Version, finding a concordance rate of 77%, suggesting that using inventories to diagnose depression is highly reliable.

- A problem in assessing the reliability of diagnosing depression over time is that patients may improve in condition between diagnoses.
- Chao-Cheng et al. (2002) raises the possibility of self-diagnosing depression by using internet self-assessments. Jürges (2008) reports that the problem with such self-assessments is that changes in self-ratings of health are underestimated by patients, reducing the reliability of such a diagnostic method.

Validity

Validity concerns how accurate, meaningful and useful diagnosis is. There are a number of ways in which validity can be assessed. For instance:

Reliability. A valid diagnosis has first to be reliable (though reliability is no guarantee of validity).

Predictive validity. If diagnosis leads to successful treatment, the diagnosis can be seen as valid.

Descriptive validity. To be valid, patients diagnosed with different disorders should actually differ from each other.

Aetiological validity. To be valid, patients diagnosed as depressed should have the same cause for their disorder.

Zigler and Phillips (1961) reported symptoms of depression to be found equally in patients assessed as neurotic and in those assessed as having bipolar disorder, as well as in 25% of diagnosed schizophrenics, implying low diagnostic validity of depression.

Sanchez-Villegas et al. (2008) assessed the validity of the Structured Clinical Interview, finding that 74.2% of depressives were accurately diagnosed, suggesting this diagnostic method to be valid.

- Validation of diagnostic scales is important in proving such criteria valid in themselves, but also because such diagnostic scales can then be used to assess further the validity of other diagnostic measures.
- A significant obstacle to the treatment of depression is the failure to diagnose symptoms. Burrows et al. (1995) found that healthcare providers under-diagnose depression in 56% of nursing home residents.

Q Explain issues associated with classification and diagnosis of depression.   *(10 marks)*

3 *Biological explanations*

Evidence from biological explanations suggests that biology underpins depression, including hereditary factors, the uniformity of symptoms across genders, ages and cultural groups, and the fact that biological therapies are effective, although environmental factors play a role too.

Genetics. Findings from twin, family, adoption and gene mapping studies suggest a genetic component, making some individuals more vulnerable than others.

Sevey et al. (2000) reviewed twin studies of bipolar disorder, finding a concordance rate of 69% in identical twins, but only 20% in non-identical twins. As MZ twins share 100% genetic similarity compared to 50% in DZ twins, this suggests a genetic influence in bipolar disorder.

Wender et al. (1986) found that adopted children who develop depression were more likely to have a biological parent with the disorder, even though adopted children are raised in a different environment, implying biological factors to be more at work than environmental ones.

Taylor et al. (1995) reviewed family studies, finding the prevalence of bipolar disorder in the general population to be 1%, while in a first-degree relative it was between 5% and 10%, implying a genetic pathway to the disorder.

Caspi et al. (2005) used gene mapping to find a relationship between depression and abnormalities in the 5-HTT gene, suggesting a genetic link. As 5-HTT is associated with the manufacture of serotonin, this implies a link between genetics and biochemical factors.

- The findings from studies involving genetics suggest evidence for the diathesis-stress model, where individuals inherit different levels of genetic predisposition to developing depression, but ultimately it is environmental triggers that determine if an individual develops the disorder.
- Twin and family studies suggest a genetic factor in the onset of depression, but often do not consider the influence that social class and sociopsychological factors between family members have.

Evolution. As depression continues to be represented in the gene pool, it is seen as having an adaptive value.

Rank theory (Price 2004) is part of the social competition hypothesis and sees depression as useful in getting an individual to admit defeat when losing a dominance fight within a social group, thus allowing individuals to realise they are trying to reach unattainable goals and not get injured.

Genome lag sees depression as a remnant of our evolutionary past, where it was once beneficial, but not as the best solution to modern-day problems.

Social navigation theory (Watson and Andrews 2002) believes that depression evolved to solve cognitively complex social problems resistant to conventional social negotiation. Depression emanates from conflict between where we are and where we wish to be, with the sobering quality of depression making us aware of necessary changes to our social network, causing us to think more systematically and to create strategies permitting goal attainment. Depression is also an honest signal of need, motivating social partners to provide support, as the depression has negative implications for their inclusive fitness: that is, 'Help me or you will lose out too.'

Shively et al. (2006) found that high-ranking monkeys had serotonin levels twice as high as other monkeys and that, if monkeys lost rank, serotonin levels fell. If given supplementary serotonin, monkeys gained rank, supporting rank theory.

Buss (1996) believes that we are more exposed to attractive people in the media than in the environment of evolutionary adaptedness (EEA), leading to feelings of inadequacy and thus depression, supporting the genome lag theory.

Hawton and Fagg (1992) found that suicide attempts of depressives stop when their relationships with close social partners improve, supporting social navigation theory.

- It is not clear if serotonin is a cause or an effect of changes in social rank and also there is a difficulty in generalising findings from research with monkeys to humans.
- Price and Sloman (1987) believe that rank theory explains depression evolving through the *yielding subroutine*, where the submissive component of ritual conflict allowed social harmony to be restored, and the *winning subroutine*, where mania evolved as the victorious component of social conflicts.

Biochemical explanations. These are centred upon the idea that abnormal levels of neurotransmitters and hormones cause depression. Attention is centred on monoamine neurotransmitters, such as serotonin, noradrenaline and dopamine, low levels having been found in depressives' brains. Anti-depressant drugs work by increasing the production of monoamines.

Certain depressions, such as post-natal depression, are also associated with hormonal changes.

Mann et al. (1996) found that major depression results from a deficiency of serotonin, or insufficient serotonin receptors, suggesting a biochemical cause to depression.

Zhou et al. (2005) found that selective serotonin reuptake inhibitors work by increasing dopamine levels in depressives, implying that the neurotransmitter is involved in the causation of depression.

Chen et al. (2006) reported that a decline in the level of the hormone insulin following childbirth might be responsible for post-natal depression.

- A problem with biochemical explanations is whether fluctuations in neurotransmitter and hormonal levels are a cause or an effect of depression.
- It may be possible to prevent post-natal depression by increasing the amount of carbohydrates eaten, as carbohydrates stimulate the production of insulin.

Q Outline and evaluate biological explanations of depression. In your evaluation you should refer to research evidence. *(25 marks)*

4 *Psychological explanations*

Although evidence indicates that biological factors play a role in the onset of depression, it is generally accepted that psychological factors are involved too.

Behaviourist explanations. Operant conditioning explains depression as being rewarding due to the attention it brings, while social learning theory sees depression occurring through observation and imitation of depressive models.

Lewinsohn (1974) proposed that depression occurs due to a decline in positive reinforcement, with individuals becoming caught in a cycle of social withdrawal, prolonging the depression.

Learned helplessness explains depression as individuals learning through experience that they cannot influence events, leading to a loss of motivation and eventually depression.

> **Maier and Seligman (1976)** found that after being placed in a situation where escape was impossible, participants did not try to escape from future similar situations where escape was possible, supporting to idea of learned helplessness.
>
> **Coleman (1986)** found that individuals receiving low rates of positive reinforcement for social behaviours become increasingly non-responsive, leading to depression, supporting Lewinsohn's theory.

- Although behaviourism explains depression as gaining the attention of others following negative events, it cannot explain why depression continues after attention declines.

Psychodynamic explanations. Freud (1917) believed that depression was related to childhood experiences of loss and that depression in adulthood was delayed regret for this loss. A child would experience anger over loss and, being unable to express this, would regress it. Similar loss in adult life would cause someone to re-experience their childhood loss.

Similarly, Bowlby (1973) thought that experiencing separation from a mother figure in early childhood led to an enhanced vulnerability to depression in later life.

> **Swaffer and Hollin (2001)** found that young offenders who repressed anger had increased vulnerability to developing depression, supporting the psychodynamic model.
>
> **Harlow et al. (1965)** found that baby monkeys separated from mothers at birth exhibited symptoms of depression, supporting the psychodynamic model.

- Psychodynamic explanations have parallels with modern theories of cognitive vulnerability, which also perceive links with experiences of loss.
- Psychodynamic theory is difficult to test scientifically and therefore difficult to refute or support.

Cognitive explanations. These see depression as resulting from cognitive vulnerabilities.

Beck (1976) explained depression as resulting from three types of negative thought patterns, which are self-defeating, resulting in depression:
- *Negative automatic thinking* — having negative thoughts about oneself, one's environment and future situations.
- *Selective attention to the negative* — paying attention to negative and not positive aspects of situations.
- *Negative self-schemas* — having a set of negative self-beliefs, influencing perception of future situations.

Abramson et al. (1989) proposed that individuals possessing a negative attributional style (attributing failures to themselves, rather than to external factors) as well as hopelessness (a belief that negative events will occur) are likely to develop depression.

Boury et al. (2001) found that depressives misinterpret facts and experiences in a negative fashion and feel hopeless about the future, supporting Beck's explanation.

Seligman (1974) reported that students making negative attributions remained depressed for longer after examinations, supporting the cognitive explanation of attributional style.

- Evidence supports the idea of cognitive vulnerability being linked to the onset of depression, with depressives selectively attending to negative stimuli.
- Evidence linking negative thinking to depression is correlational and thus does not show causality.

Sociocultural explanations. These focus upon the effect that life events, in the form of stressors, have upon the onset and maintenance of depression.

Focus has also fallen upon the role that social networks play, especially whether people with reduced social support are vulnerable to depression, with a possible link to the level of social and interpersonal skills that individuals possess.

Leavey et al. (2007) found Irish migrants to Britain vulnerable to depression, with the origins of depression often located in difficult life events, supporting the sociocultural viewpoint.

- The sociocultural viewpoint can explain differences in prevalence rates between ethnic, gender and socioeconomic groups: for instance, women being more likely to develop depression due to having more life event stressors.

Q Outline and evaluate two psychological explanations for depression. *(25 marks)*

5 *Biological therapies*

The two common biological treatments for depression are drugs and ECT, with psychosurgery used in severe non-responsive cases incurring a high risk of death by suicide. Seasonal affective disorder has been successfully treated with *light therapy*, involving the use of bright full-spectrum lights at particular times of day. This treatment is often used in conjunction with drugs.

Drug treatment

Anti-depressant drugs stimulate the production of monoamine neurotransmitters, leading to increased physical arousal.

Old-fashioned anti-depressants, such as monoamine oxidase inhibitors, stop serotonin, noradrenaline and dopamine being broken down, so their levels are increased, while tricyclics stop serotonin and noradrenaline being reabsorbed, so again their levels are increased.

Effective in treating depression, anti-depressants can incur side-effects, such as drowsiness.

Modern anti-depressants affect the level of one monoamine, such as prozac, preventing serotonin being reabsorbed or broken down. There is no best drug, patients tending to respond differently to different drugs, with drug choice also affected by symptoms displayed and side-effects exhibited.

Furukawa et al. (2003) reviewed 35 studies, finding anti-depressants more effective than placebos, suggesting that anti-depressants are an effective treatment

Kirsch (2008) found that the new generation of anti-depressants work no better than a placebo for most patients and accused drug companies of suppressing research evidence casting doubt on these drugs' effectiveness.

- Anti-depressant drugs are cost-effective, occur in tablet form — a familiar and trusted form of treatment — and have the added benefit of being self-administered.
- Research indicates that psychological treatments are more effective than anti-depressants, but such treatments are not favoured as they are more costly.

Electro-convulsive therapy

Electro-convulsive therapy (ECT) produces a seizure lasting up to a minute. Bilateral shocks, to both sides of the head, are more effective than unilateral shocks to one side of the head, but produce more side-effects. Modern forms of ECT use mild shocks for very brief periods, with ECT generally administered two or three times a week for about eight treatments, along with an anaesthetic and a muscle relaxant to prevent bone fractures.

ECT is controversial, as it can seem brutal and has side-effects such as temporary memory loss, which get more severe as treatments continue. It is not completely clear how ECT works, but modern forms are more humane and are deemed appropriate when other treatments have failed, or when a patient is perceived as a suicide risk.

Paguin et al. (2008) performed a meta-analysis of ECT, comparing studies of ECT, placebos and anti-depressant drugs. They found ECT superior, suggesting that it is a valid therapeutic tool for treating depression, including severe and resistant forms.

Levy (1968) compared bilateral with unilateral forms of ECT, finding that unilateral treatments incurred less memory loss, but bilateral treatments produced better relief of depressive symptoms.

- The side-effects of ECT are more severe with children, adolescents, the elderly and pregnant women, and therefore should not be used as a treatment for these categories of people, unless as a last resort.
- There is a high relapse rate associated with ECT. Sackheim et al. (2001) found that 84% of patients relapsed within 6 months, implying the treatment to be ineffective in the long term.

Q Outline and evaluate one biological therapy for the treatment of depression. Refer to research evidence in your answer.

(10 marks)

6 *Psychological therapies*

Behaviourist treatments see depression as a learned behaviour, and so use reinforcements to elevate mood and encourage positive behaviours. Social reinforcement, in the form of family members and social networks, are utilised to provide support.

Behavioural activation therapy (BAT) perceives depression as an indication of things in an individual's life that need to change. Exercises aiding concentration on activities bringing feelings of joy and mastery are used, and a schedule of activities is built up to create a normal and satisfying life.

Social skills training (SST) operates on the principle that when patients improve social skills, their levels of self-esteem increase and others respond favourably to them. Patients are taught to alter behaviour patterns by practising selected behaviours in individual or group therapy sessions.

Houghton et al. (2008) found BAT to be effective and tolerable, with a low-drop out rate.

La Fromboise and Rowe (1983) found that structured learning therapy, based on social skills training, improved the psychosocial functioning of males and females of varying age groups and ethnic backgrounds, and proved effective in treating those who found psychotherapy difficult.

- BAT can be successfully modified for use with different groups of patients with very different needs, such as the elderly or adolescents, emphasising its effectiveness.
- SST is problematic in generalising newly learned social skills to real-life situations. Generalisation occurs better when SST has a clear focus and patients are motivated to reach realistic goals, with suitable skills being taught for specific patients.

Psychodynamic therapy

The roots of depression are seen as occurring in childhood; therefore psychodynamic therapy explores a patient's past, linking this to their current situation, with childhood experiences of loss and rejection especially crucial to depression. Patients are encouraged to relive experiences and gain insight into their inability to form healthy relationships, especially the transference of anger incurred from early rejection and loss on to others.

Leichsenring et al. (2004) found brief dynamic therapy, a simpler form of psychodynamic treatment, to be as effective as CBT in addressing depression.

De Clerq et al. (1999) found psychodynamic psychotherapy to be a desirable and feasible treatment, when delivered by skilled, well-trained nurses under close supervision, suggesting that the treatment's effectiveness is dependent upon the quality of the clinicians administering it.

- Psychotherapy works best when patients attend all scheduled sessions, which requires motivation and effort, not always easy to achieve with those exhibiting symptoms of depression.
- Eysenck (1952) found that only 44% of patients improved with psychotherapy, compared to 66% of patients who got better without any form of treatment, suggesting that psychotherapy is less effective than no treatment at all.

Cognitive-behavioural therapy

The idea behind cognitive-behavioural therapy (CBT) is that beliefs, expectations and cognitive assessments of self, the environment and the nature of personal problems affect how a person perceives themselves and others, how problems are approached and how successful a person is in coping and attaining goals.

CBT assists patients in identifying irrational and maladaptive thoughts and altering them. Thoughts affect emotions and thus behaviour, and it is the patient's thinking that has to be altered for reduction of depression symptoms to occur. Drawings are employed to display links between thoughts, actions and emotions, with comprehension of where symptoms come from being useful in reducing anxiety levels.

Flannaghan et al. (1997) found CBT to be effective in treating depressive stroke victims, suggesting that it is a suitable treatment for specific groups of depressives.

Whitfield and Williams (2003) found CBT to have the strongest research base for effectiveness, but recognised that there was a cost problem in delivering weekly face-to-face sessions for patients on the National Health Service.

- CBT is regarded as the most effective psychological treatment for moderate and severe depression and one of the most effective treatments where depression is the main problem.
- One of the advantages of CBT as a general treatment of depression, compared to other forms of treatment, is that it produces little in the way of side-effects.

Q Outline and evaluate two or more psychological therapies for the treatment of depression.

(25 marks)

C Anxiety disorders

Two anxiety disorders — phobic disorders and obsessive-compulsive disorder — are presented here, but only one needs to be covered to guarantee being able to answer any examination question on anxiety disorders.

1 Clinical characteristics

One in five people experience anxiety levels so high that they become maladaptive and negatively affect day-to-day functioning.

Phobic disorders are characterised by extreme, irrational and enduring fears that cannot be controlled, involving anxiety levels beyond any actual risk.

Phobic disorders are twice as common among females, with 10% of the population suffering from a specific phobia at some point. Most phobias originate in childhood and diminish in strength during adulthood.

Obsessive-compulsive disorder (OCD) occurs in 2% of the population, sufferers enduring persistent and intrusive thoughts occurring as obsessions, compulsions or a combination of both.

Obsessions consist of forbidden or inappropriate ideas and visual images leading to feelings of anxiety, whereas compulsions consist of intense, uncontrollable urges to perform tasks and behaviours repetitively, such as constantly cleaning. Sufferers realise their compulsions are inappropriate, but cannot exert control over them, resulting in greater levels of anxiety.

Both phobias and OCD are exaggerated versions of normal behaviour and are perceived as mental disorders when they become detrimental to everyday functioning.

Symptoms — phobic disorders

Persistent, excessive fear — high anxiety due to the presence or anticipation of feared situations.

Fear from exposure to phobic stimulus — immediate fear response, even panic attack, due to the presentation of phobic situations.

Recognition of exaggerated anxiety — the sufferer is aware that the level of anxiety is overstated.

Avoidant/anxiety response — feared situations are avoided or lead to high anxiety response.

Disruption of functioning — the anxiety/avoidance response is so extreme that it interferes with the ability to conduct everyday working and social functioning.

Sub-types

Phobias are divisible into (1) *simple phobias*, where sufferers fear specific situations (e.g. *pediophobia*, a fear of dolls); and (2) *social phobias*, where sufferers fear social environments (e.g. talking in public).

Social phobias can be further divided into:
- *animal phobias* (e.g. arachnophobia, fear of spiders)
- *injury phobias* (e.g. hematophobia, fear of blood)
- *situational phobias* (e.g. aerophobia, fear of flying)
- *natural environment phobias* (e.g. hydrophobia, fear of water)

Symptoms — OCD

Obsessions. These are:
- *Recurrent and persistent.* Inappropriate and intrusive thoughts, impulses and images are recurrently experienced, leading to anxiety and distress.
- *Irrelevant to real life.* Thoughts, impulses and images experienced are not relevant to real-life situations.
- *Suppressed.* Sufferers attempt to suppress thoughts, impulses and images with alternative thoughts or actions.
- *Recognised as self-generated.* Sufferers recognise that obsessional thoughts, impulses and images are a product of their own invention and not inserted externally.

Compulsions. These are:
- *Repetitive.* Sufferers feel compelled to repeat behaviours and mental acts in response to obsessional thoughts, impulses and images.
- *Aimed at reducing distress.* Behaviours and mental acts are an attempt to reduce distress or prevent feared events, although they have little realistic chance of doing so.

Other symptoms. Symptoms are:
- *Recognised as excessive.* Sufferers realise that obsessions/compulsions are excessive.
- *Time consuming.* Obsessions/compulsions are time consuming, cause distress and interfere with everyday working and social functioning.
- *Unrelated to substance abuse.* OCD is not related to substance abuse or other medical conditions.

Q Outline the clinical characteristics of one anxiety disorder. *(9 marks)*

2 Issues surrounding classification and diagnosis

Reliability

This refers to the consistency of measurements and affects classification and diagnosis of anxiety disorders in two ways:
- *Test–retest reliability* occurs when a practitioner makes consistent diagnoses on separate occasions from the same information.
- *Inter-rater reliability* occurs when several practitioners make identical, independent diagnoses of the same patient.

Phobias

Silverman et al. (2001) examined the test–retest reliability of phobic disorders in children aged between 7 and 16 years old. The Anxiety Disorders Interview Schedule for DSM IV was administered twice, results indicating reliability for simple and social phobias

Alstrom et al. (2009) assessed the inter-rater reliability of phobic disorder diagnosis in Swedish patients, finding inter-rater reliability to be very good with a 90% concurrence rate.

- Assessment of inter-rater reliability involves one rater interviewing a patient and another observing the interview. Therefore, both diagnoses are based on identical information and, not surprisingly, show high reliability. Far better is for one rater to perform an interview and the second rater to perform a separate independent interview on the same patient.
- Research studies differ in the assessment of reliability even when identical measuring scales are used. Early assessments of the Anxiety Disorder Interview Schedule found low reliability for phobic disorders, while later studies found higher levels, suggesting that it is the revision of measuring scales that led to improved reliability of diagnosis.

OCD

Di Nardo and Barlow (1987) found that the principal diagnosis of OCD was associated with excellent diagnostic reliability, scoring an 80% concurrence rate, second only to simple phobias among anxiety and mood disorders.

Foa et al. (1987), using Likert scales, obtained large correlations among patients', therapists' and independent observers' ratings of OCD features, including main fear, avoidance and compulsion severity. This suggests good inter-rater reliability.

- The high prevalence of OCD and its secretive nature, leading to under-recognition of the disorder, suggests the need for a simple, quick reliable diagnostic tool to identify cases.
- The fact that OCD has easily observable symptoms assists clear diagnosis of the disorder, which contributes to high levels of reliability.

Validity

Validity concerns how accurate, meaningful and useful diagnosis is. There are a number of ways in which validity can be assessed. For instance:

Reliability. A valid diagnosis has first to be reliable (though reliability itself is no guarantee of validity).

Predictive validity. If diagnosis leads to successful treatment, the diagnosis can be seen as valid.

Descriptive validity. For the diagnosis to be valid, patients diagnosed with different disorders should actually differ from each other.

Aetiological validity. For the diagnosis to be valid, patients diagnosed with anxiety disorders should have the same cause for their disorder.

Phobias

Herbert et al. (1992) assessed the descriptive validity of social phobias, comparing them with avoidant personality disorder (APD). They found social phobias and APD to represent quantitatively, but not qualitatively, distinct disorders, suggesting that social phobias are not a separate disorder.

Vasey and Dadds (2001) tested the predictive validity of anxiety disorder diagnoses. They found few differences in treatment outcomes for different sub-groups, suggesting low predictive validity.

- The predictive validity of diagnostic systems relating to children's anxiety disorders has been subject to little research, and studies assessed indicate little evidence of childhood anxiety disorders predicting different outcomes, suggesting low predictive validity.
- Rabung et al. (2009) believe that self-rating instruments can be valid measuring tools of phobias, as they are sensitive to change, suitable for clinical use and cost-effective, because they can be downloaded free from the internet.

OCD

Leckman and Chittenden (1990), assessing the validity of diagnosis of OCD, found that 50% of patients with Tourette's syndrome also had OCD, indicating OCD not to be a separate disorder.

Deacon and Abramovitz (2004) tested the validity of the Yale–Brown Obsessive Compulsive Scale, regarded as the gold-standard measure of OCD, by applying it to patients with a diagnosis of OCD. They found problems with the ability to measure the components of OCD validly, suggesting that the scale needs serious revision.

- Diagnoses of OCD have a long-term impact on sufferers' lives and yet such diagnoses are made with little evidence of the disorder existing as a separate condition.
- Although evidence indicates that many measuring scales used to assess OCD are not valid, they are still regarded as the most effective assessment tool in determining diagnostic and treatment outcomes.

Q To what extent are diagnoses of anxiety disorders valid?   *(25 marks)*

3   *Biological explanations*

Genetics

Results from twin and family studies indicate some genetic influence on anxiety disorders, although it is difficult to separate out environmental influences.

Gene mapping studies involve comparing genetic material from families with a high and low incidence of anxiety disorders. Results indicate that particular genes are involved, making some individuals more vulnerable than others.

Phobias

Kendler et al. (1992) found a 24% concordance rate for social phobia in identical female twins, compared to 15% for non-identical female twins, suggesting a genetic influence.

Reich and Yates (1988) found social phobia rates higher in relatives of social phobics (6%) than in relatives of non-social phobic controls (2%), suggesting some genetic influence.

Gelertner et al. (2004) conducted a gene mapping study on sufferers of social phobias, finding a link to social phobias for various markers of chromosome 16, with additional interest also centred on chromosomes 9, 14 and 18. This suggests evidence of a genetic component.

- The onset of phobic disorders may involve the diathesis-stress model, where individuals inherit different degrees of vulnerability, but it is environmental triggers that ultimately determine if an individual goes on to develop the disorder.
- Although evidence from twin and family studies suggests a genetic influence, it may be that related individuals acquire phobias through similar environmental experiences, or through imitation.

OCD

Grootheest et al. (2005) reviewed 70 years of twin studies into OCD, finding a heritability rate of up to 65% for OCD in children and 47% in adults. This suggests a genetic contribution.

Lenane et al. (1990) studied the prevalence of OCD among related family members, finding evidence for heritability. This supports the genetic viewpoint.

Samuels et al. (2007) used gene mapping to compare OCD sufferers exhibiting hoarding behaviour with OCD sufferers who did not, finding a link to chromosome 14 marker D14S588. This suggests a genetic influence and may also indicate the existence of separate OCD sub-types.

- Weissman (1985) noted that the tendency for OCD to run in families was first observed over a century ago, therefore such an idea is not new and has influenced subsequent research.
- The fact that family members often display dissimilar OCD symptoms, such as a child arranging dolls and an adult constantly washing dishes, weakens support for the genetic viewpoint, as if the disorder was inherited, exhibited behaviours would be the same.

Evolutionary explanations

Anxiety disorders continue to be apparent in the population, suggesting an adaptive value.

Biological preparedness is the idea that animals have an innate ability to display certain fears and therefore develop some conditioned fears easily. Such fears are genetic and environmental, as the phobia has to be learned from environmental experience, with the predisposition to learn the fear being the inherited component.

Phobias serve several adaptive functions, such as the fear element of a phobia freezing an individual on the spot, aiding concealment from predators, or the flight response helping to outrun predators. Alternatively, fear bends individuals into submission against dominant aggressors, saving them from harm. The fear response may even release hormones aiding the clotting of blood to help heal wounds and stimulate the liver to release glucose for energy, which is important to facilitate 'flight or fight'.

OCD often involves repetitive behaviours, such as washing, and these would have been important in our evolutionary past in preventing infection. Similar behaviours may have increased vigilance and alertness, incurring a survival value. Modern-day versions, such as continually cleaning handles, are an exaggeration of ancient adaptations.

Phobias

Cook and Mineka (1989) demonstrated to laboratory-raised monkeys the fear response of a wild monkey to a snake and a rabbit. Subsequently, the laboratory-raised monkeys showed a similar response to a toy snake, but not a toy rabbit, suggesting an evolutionary readiness to fear snakes, but not rabbits.

Bennett-Levy and Marteau (1984) got participants to rate animals for ugliness, fearfulness and harmfulness. The less human an animal appeared, the bigger the fear response, suggesting an adaptive readiness to fear certain things more than others.

- Learned helplessness explains why it is harder to develop fears of dangerous modern-day objects and situations, such as guns, because they were not around in the EEA and are not coded into our genes.
- Some phobias are so bizarre and individual that they are better explained as purely conditioned responses, rather than having an evolved component.

OCD

Marks and Nesse (1984) state that a lack of concern for others incurs a risk of ostracism from social groups, so the fact that OCD sufferers are concerned for the welfare of others reduces the risk, suggesting an adaptive value.

Chepko-Sade et al. (1989) found that rhesus monkeys performing the most grooming of others were retained within the group following group in-fighting, suggesting that OCD tends to have an adaptive value.

- Behavioural features of OCD, such as hoarding, were beneficial to hunting and gathering food in our evolutionary past and remain now due to genome lag, where genes take time to evolve and better fit the current environment.
- Evolutionary explanations of OCD do not account for individual and cultural differences.

Biochemical explanations

Although not a sole explanation of anxiety disorders, biochemical factors may play a part in determining levels of vulnerability.

The amino acid GABA has been indicated as involved in the control of arousal and anxiety levels by suppressing nervous system activity, making a person feel less anxious. Certain individuals appear to be more susceptible to environmental influences and have above average levels of physical arousal and anxiety, reflecting abnormal GABA functioning.

Abnormal neurotransmitter activity is associated with OCD, attention being especially directed at reduced levels of serotonin and elevated levels of dopamine.

Phobias

Sahley (2001) reports that social phobics have an altered brain structure characterised by low serotonin levels and an overactive limbic system. When given amino acids like GABA, symptoms lessen, supporting the biochemical explanation.

Benjamin et al. (2000) gave phobics serotonin-enhancing drugs, finding that symptoms were reduced, suggesting a link between phobias and reduced serotonin functioning.

- The successful treatment of phobias with GABA and selective serotonin re-uptake inhibitors (SS-RIs) provide strong evidence of a role for biochemistry in the development of phobias.
- Evidence suggests that phobias do not occur due to low serotonin functioning, but low serotonin functioning makes people more susceptible to becoming phobic due to environmental factors.

OCD

Fineberg (1996) found that the symptoms of OCD were reduced in patients taking SSRIs, which increase levels of serotonin in the brain, while **Hollander et al. (1988)** found that symptoms worsen with serotonin agonists, which reduce serotonin levels, lending support to the serotonin hypothesis.

Insel et al. (1991) reported on three drugs — clomipramine, prozac and fluvoxamine — all of which stimulate serotonin production and benefit OCD patients, supporting the biochemical explanation.

- Psychological treatments for OCD have proven successful and do not elevate serotonin levels in doing so, reducing support for the serotonin hypothesis.
- Even where evidence links biochemistry to OCD, it is not clear whether biochemical factors are a cause or an effect of the disorder.

Q **(a)** Outline two biological explanations of one anxiety disorder. *(9 marks)*

  (b) Evaluate one of the biological explanations of one anxiety disorder outlined
    in (a). *(16 marks)*

4 *Psychological explanations*

There are several psychological explanations of anxiety disorders, including behaviourist, cognitive, psychodynamic and sociocultural explanations. Evidence indicates that biological factors play an important role, but psychological factors are involved too.

Behaviourist explanations

Classical conditioning explains phobias as occurring through the association of traumatic events with neutral stimuli and the resulting phobias becoming resistant to extinction, because of avoidance responses made to avoid feared situations.

Operant conditioning explains how phobias are maintained, as when avoidance responses are made; the fear element is reduced, reinforcing the avoidance responses and making them likely to recur.

Operant conditioning also explains the maintenance of OCD, as when a sufferer experiences anxiety, for instance about infection, and washing door handles is reinforcing, as it reduces anxiety, making the behaviour likely to recur.

Social learning theory explains phobias as occurring through observation and imitation of others. Merely watching someone experience trauma causes the observer to experience the fear response in the presence of the same stimulus.

Phobias

Watson and Rayner (1920) conditioned 'Little Albert' to fear white furry objects by pairing the neutral stimulus of a white rat with the unconditioned stimulus of a loud noise, producing an innate fear response, demonstrating how phobias can be learned by classical conditioning.

Gray (1975) used the *two-process theory* to explain how operant conditioning can strengthen phobias acquired through classical conditioning. A phobia is first learned by a specific event being paired with the fear response, and then an avoidance response is learned that reduces the fear element, thus strengthening the avoidance response.

Ost and Hugdahl (1981) reported on a boy witnessing his grandfather vomit while dying and subsequently developing a persistent vomiting phobia, supporting the social learning explanation.

- The success of behaviourist treatments, such as systematic desensitisation, in addressing phobic symptoms lends support to behaviourist explanations.
- The behaviourist viewpoint is weakened by the fact that not everyone experiencing traumatic events goes on to develop phobias.

OCD

Meyer and Cheeser (1970) demonstrated how compulsions are learnt responses reducing heightened anxiety levels brought on by obsessions, providing a behaviourist explanation for elements of the disorder.

Einstein and Menzies (2003) found a relationship between OCD symptoms and magical thinking, suggesting a link between superstition and OCD. This supports Skinner's (1948) *superstition hypothesis*, where bodily actions become repeated due to an association with a reinforcer.

- Schwartz et al. (1996) reported behavioural therapies effective in reducing symptoms of OCD and incurring changes in biochemical activity, supporting the behaviourist explanation.
- Although certain features of OCD can be explained by behaviourism, intrusive thoughts, a key feature of the disorder, cannot, weakening the explanation.

Psychodynamic explanations

Phobias are seen as an *ego defence* mechanism that helps cope with repressed anxieties by becoming displaced on to phobic objects symbolising the initial conflict.

Bowlby (1973) saw early attachment experiences as involved with the formation of phobias due to children experiencing separation anxiety, or having over-protective parents.

OCD is perceived as occurring in those who demonstrate anal personality characteristics, such as being very tidy, organised and punctual, and thus OCD is an exaggeration of the anal personality type.

Obsessions are also seen as *defence mechanisms* occupying the mind to displace threatening thoughts:
- *Isolation* — the ego separates itself from unacceptable urges, though still having an effect as obsessional thoughts.
- *Undoing* — the ego copes with anxiety by developing compulsive behaviours that symbolically deconstruct unacceptable urges.
- *Reaction formation* — anxiety is reduced by enacting behaviours that are the opposite of the unacceptable urges.

Phobias

Knijnik et al. (2004) gave psychodynamic group therapy to patients with social phobias, and found that their condition improved, supporting the psychodynamic explanation.

Salzman (1980) found that psychodynamic therapies are of little help to clients with phobias and OCD, but of more help to those with general anxiety disorders, implying that the psychodynamic approach cannot explain phobias or OCD.

- The psychodynamic approach is based upon case studies, therefore the results from one person may not be generalisable to others.
- The psychodynamic approach focuses upon symbolic meanings of phobic objects, rather than empirically based evidence, weakening support for the explanation.

OCD

Petersen (1992) found no support for the idea that people with obsessive personality styles are more likely to develop OCD, weakening support for the explanation.

Noonan (1971) found that psychoanalysis worsens OCD symptoms because clients tend to be anxious about their condition, weakening the psychodynamic argument.

- Adler (1931) presented an alternative psychodynamic explanation for OCD, seeing the condition as arising from experiencing feelings of insecurity, inferiority and incompetence.
- The psychodynamic approach sees the roots of OCD as contained within childhood. However, Freud only presented one case study of a child — 'Little Hans' — and this study was actually carried out by the boy's father, which weakens the explanation.

Cognitive explanations

Phobias are seen as originating from maladaptive thinking, occurring as a reaction to anxiety-generating situations.

OCD is seen as originating from sufferers having impaired, persistent thought processes. These types of thinking lead to self-blame, depression and heightened anxiety. Behaviours that lessen impaired, obsessive thoughts become compulsive because of their anxiety-reducing qualities, and become difficult to control.

Another cognitive factor concerns the tendency of people with anxiety disorders to be affected by *attentional bias*, such as phobics concentrating more attention than other people on anxiety-generating stimuli.

Thorpe and Salkovskis (2000) assessed conscious beliefs related to exposure to phobic stimuli, finding a major role in specific phobias for thoughts related to harm. This suggests that specific phobias are cognitive in origin.

Kindt and Brosschot (1997) found that arachnophobics took longer to name the ink colour of spider-related words on a Stroop test, supporting the cognitive explanation.

- The cognitive explanation is deterministic, as it perceives phobias as being caused by psychological factors over which sufferers have no control.
- The cognitive viewpoint explains how phobias are maintained, but not why they originate. A phobia could be caused by conditioning or genetics and then be perpetuated by faulty thinking

OCD

Davison and Neale (1994) found that OCD patients cannot distinguish between imagination and reality, supporting the idea of faulty thinking processes being linked to OCD.

Clark (1992) reported that intrusive thinking is more common in OCD sufferers than in the normal population, supporting the cognitive argument.

- Cognitive treatments of OCD have proved effective by correcting cognitive bias and helping sufferers to become less vigilant, providing support for the cognitive explanation.
- The cognitive explanation does not explain the emotional aspect of irrational beliefs, weakening support for the viewpoint.

Sociocultural factors

Some phobias occur more in some cultures, and certain phobias are culture-specific, implying a cultural influence, while OCD occurs in a remarkably similar fashion and prevalence across cultures, suggesting that cultural factors do not play a large role. However, culture can affect actual symptoms displayed, which tend to reflect the characteristics of a given culture.

Social factors concern the role that family dynamics play in developing anxiety disorders, such as fearful and socially anxious parents unknowingly transferring information to children about the dangers of social situations and the children developing the same anxiety themselves.

Phobias

Kleinknecht et al. (1997) reported on Taijin Kyofusho, a Japanese social phobia where sufferers fear offending others with inappropriate behaviour, suggesting that some phobias are culturally determined.

Bruch and Heimberg (1994) found that children of socially isolated parents tend to be more socially isolated themselves and therefore more at risk of developing social phobias.

- The fact that children of parents with an anxiety disorder are at risk of developing the disorder themselves is as easily explained in genetic terms as by social factors.
- Media emphasis on demonstrating 'normal' and 'attractive' personal characteristics may contribute to individuals feeling inferior and insecure, and developing social phobias.

OCD

Fontenelle et al. (2004) found that obsessions centred on aggression and religious observations were common in Brazilian and middle eastern populations, implying that OCD symptoms take on the characteristics of a given culture.

Jaisoorya et al. (2008) found that male OCD sufferers had an earlier onset of the disorder and more religious obsessions, while females had more cleaning and hair-pulling compulsions, suggesting social factors to be involved.

- The fact that prevalence rates of OCD are similar cross-culturally suggests that biological factors may be involved.
- The prevalence rate of OCD is similar for males and females, suggesting that biological factors are involved.

Q Outline and evaluate psychological explanations of one anxiety disorder.   *(25 marks)*

5 *Biological therapies*

Drugs

Anxiolytics, such as the benzodiazepines (BZs), work by increasing the effect of the neurotransmitter GABA and reduce anxiety in phobics and OCD sufferers. There can be side-effects, though, such as drowsiness.

Phobics and OCD sufferers are also treated with anti-depressants. SSRIs elevate serotonin levels, while monoamine oxidase inhibitors (MAOIs) increase serotonin and noradrenaline levels.

Anti-psychotic drugs, with a dopamine-lowering effect, are also useful in treating OCD.

Beta-blockers have had success in reducing physical symptoms of anxiety disorders. They work by countering the rises in blood pressure and heart rate associated with anxiety, by lowering adrenaline and noradrenaline production.

Phobias

Slaap et al. (1996) treated social phobics with anti-depressant SSRIs, finding that 72% of patients had reductions in heart rate and blood pressure, suggesting drug treatments to be effective in addressing physical symptoms of the disorder.

Den Boer et al. (1994) found MAOIs, such as moclobemide, to be effective in reducing social anxiety and social avoidance, although there is an increased risk of hypertension.

- Aside from their addictive qualities, another problem with BZs is that once a patient stops taking them, they can experience a sharp rise again in anxiety levels.
- Drug treatments have proved effective in reducing physical symptoms of phobias so that psychological treatments can be effectively applied.

OCD

Beroqvist et al. (1999) investigated the effect of low doses of the anti-psychotic drug risperidone in treating OCD, finding treatment effective due to the drug's dopamine-lowering effect.

Flament et al. (1985) tested the anti-depressant drug clomipramine's ability to address symptoms of childhood OCD, finding it to be superior to placebo treatment, supporting the use of drug treatments.

- Drug treatments are not a cure for OCD, as once drug taking stops, symptoms reappear.
- Drug treatments are widely used to treat OCD as they are a cost-effective and user-friendly form of treatment.

Psychosurgery

Psychosurgery is occasionally used for severe cases of anxiety disorders that are unresponsive to other treatments. It is a last resort, entailing the usual risks of surgery, involves irreversible destruction of tissue without any guarantee of success and can incur serious side-effects, such as reduced intellect.

Certain criteria must be met before psychosurgery is considered:
- There must be clinical diagnosis of an anxiety disorder.
- Symptoms must be severe, obstructing purposeful everyday living.
- Other treatments must have failed.
- The patient must give fully informed consent, with full knowledge of the procedure and risks involved.

Psychosurgery involves drilling holes in the skull so that heated probes can be inserted to burn away specific, small areas of brain tissue.

Phobias

Ruck et al. (2003) reported that patients who had capsulotomies performed for severe social phobias generally had large reductions in anxiety levels, demonstrating the technique to be effective, although some patients suffered severe side-effects.

Balon (2003) reported that thermocapsulotomy can be an effective treatment for cases of acute phobias, but is an extreme option, again carrying a risk of severe side-effects.

- It seems improbable that different mental symptoms can be relieved by one single form of brain operation, and therefore only operations suitable for precise psychiatric diagnoses should be used.
- Modern forms of psychosurgery are targeted on localised, specific brain areas, therefore avoiding large-scale destruction and reducing risks of irreversible side-effects.

OCD

> **Kelly and Cobb (1985)** reported that 78% of patients suffering from OCD displayed improved symptoms 20 months after limbic leucotomies were performed, suggesting support for the treatment.
>
> **Hindus et al. (1985)** followed up gamma capsulotomy surgical cases 3 and 7 years after treatment, finding that only a few OCD patients showed improvements. This suggests that different forms of psychosurgery have vastly different success rates.

- Psychosurgery is only used after a patient gives fully informed consent. However, it is debatable whether someone with severe OCD can actually give fully informed consent, suggesting that there may be ethical problems in administering the treatment.
- Psychosurgery cannot be considered a cure for OCD, as patients undergoing neurosurgery continue to need psychiatric care.

Q Outline and evaluate one biological therapy for the treatment of one anxiety disorder. Refer to research evidence in your answer. *(20 marks)*

6 *Psychological therapies*

Behavioural therapy

Systematic desensitisation (SD) is the main behaviourist treatment for phobias. SD is based on classical conditioning, patients learning in stages to associate phobic situations with feelings of calm rather than fear. The idea is that it is not possible for the two opposing emotions of anxiety and relaxation to exist together (*reciprocal inhibition*).

A hierarchy is drawn up before treatment commences, going from least to most feared type of contact with the phobic situation, the patient being taught relaxation strategies to use at each stage. Contact is achieved by imagining the scenario (*covert desensitisation*) or having actual contact (*in vivo desensitisation*).

Implosion (*flooding*) is where patients go straight to the top of the hierarchy and imagine, or have direct contact with, the most feared scenario. The idea is that patients are not allowed to make avoidance responses and therefore anxiety peaks at such a level that it cannot be maintained.

SD is used against OCD, sufferers being introduced to the situations causing their obsessions and, by using relaxation strategies, lowering anxiety levels.

Another treatment for OCD is *exposure and response prevention* (ERP), where sufferers are introduced to situations causing their obsessions, but are not allowed to make obsessive responses. If OCD has occurred through reinforcement, avoiding anxiety-creating scenarios means that reinforcement is prevented and relearning can occur.

Phobias

> **Rothbaum et al. (1998)** reported on virtual reality exposure therapy where patients are active participants within a computer-generated three-dimensional world that changes naturally with head movements. SD-like treatment occurs without ever leaving the therapist's office, more control is gained over phobic stimuli and there is less exposure of the patient to harm and embarrassment.
>
> **Wolpe (1960)** used implosion to remove a girl's phobia of driving in cars. The girl was forced into a car and driven around for hours until her hysteria had subsided, demonstrating the effectiveness of the treatment.

- SD is suitable for patients who are able to use relaxation strategies and have imaginations vivid enough to conjure up images of feared situations.
- Although patients may be able gradually to confront phobias in an imaginary sense, there is no guarantee that this will work with the actual situation, which is why *in vivo* treatment is thought superior to covert desensitisation.

OCD

Gertz (1966) reported that *in vivo* SD worked well with OCD patients. They found that 66% of sufferers responded to treatment, suggesting the treatment to be effective.

Baer (1991) found that a self-directed, step-by-step form of ERP was as effective for mild forms of OCD as seeing a therapist, and therefore is considered cost-effective.

- ERP incurs large dropout rates due to high levels of anxiety, therefore it is usually combined with drug treatment so that anxiety levels can be controlled.
- ERP is considered more effective than drug treatments, as relapse rates are much lower, suggesting that ERP brings long-term, lasting benefits.

Psychodynamic therapies

Psychodynamic therapies try to reveal the repressed childhood conflicts expressed as phobias, so the sufferer has insight into the origins of their disorder and eventually arrives at a more rational understanding of events occurring in their past.

Before the introduction of other types of treatments and therapies, psychoanalysis was often used as a treatment for OCD and, indeed, it is considered a useful means of addressing the condition, as sufferers often have a degree of insight into their condition.

Phobias

Knijnik et al. (2004) gave psychodynamic group therapy for 12 weeks to patients with social phobias, finding that their condition improved, supporting the psychodynamic explanation.

Klein et al. (1983) reported that psychodynamic psychotherapy for specific phobias was as effective as *in vivo* behaviourist treatments, indicating the worth of psychodynamically based treatments.

- The psychodynamic approach to treating phobias works in association with cognitive and humanistic, behavioural and social therapies, demonstrating its flexibility and range of use.
- Psychodynamic therapies are suitable for use with children, adolescents and adults.

OCD

Gava et al. (2009) attempted to review different biological and psychological treatments for OCD, but were unable to assess psychodynamic treatments due to a lack of evidence, suggesting that the treatment has become obsolete.

Greist and Jefferson (2007) reported that psychodynamic psychotherapy and psychoanalysis have not been effective for people with OCD, weakening support for such treatments.

- Although psychoanalysis seems appropriate for OCD because sufferers have insight into their condition, insight alone is not enough to eradicate the disorder, suggesting it to be largely biological in nature.
- Unlike cognitive-behavioural therapies developed solely for OCD, there are no psychodynamic treatments designed specifically to combat the disorder.

Cognitive-behavioural therapy

Cognitive-behavioural therapy (CBT) is the most frequently used treatment for phobias and OCD.

CBT helps patients identify irrational and maladaptive thinking patterns and change them to rational, adaptive ones. Thinking underpins feelings and behaviour, so by changing modes of thinking, feelings and behaviour also change. The drawing of diagrams demonstrating links between thinking, emotions and behaviour is used to facilitate this process.

For patients with, for example, snake phobias, the therapist encourages phobics to express beliefs about snakes and then challenges these with rational arguments. Patients are encouraged to interact with snakes and record details that can be referred to if sufferers return to their irrational beliefs.

Cognitive-behavioural group therapy is a form of CBT used with phobics, where group members support sufferers as they work through a hierarchy of fears, using relaxation strategies at each step. The cognitive element of the treatment involves replacing irrational beliefs generating anxiety with rational ones. Phobic situations are enacted, group members challenging each other's irrational beliefs.

With OCD, CBT is orientated at changing obsessional thinking, such as with *habituation training*, where sufferers relive obsessional thoughts repeatedly to reduce the anxiety created.

Phobias

Spence et al. (2000) assessed the value of CBT in children with social phobias, finding child-focused CBT and CBT plus parental involvement effective in reducing social and general anxiety levels, with these improvements apparent at a 1-year follow-up. This suggests that CBT has long-term effectiveness with phobic children.

Kvale et al. (2004) conducted a meta-analysis of treatment studies for people with dental phobias, finding that CBT resulted in 77% of patients regularly visiting a dentist 4 years after treatment.

- There are long-term benefits to CBT, as the techniques used to combat phobias can be used continually to help stop symptoms returning.
- One of the advantages of CBT compared to other treatments is that it produces little in the way of side-effects.

OCD

O'Kearney et al. (2006) assessed the ability of CBT to treat children and adolescents with OCD, finding it effective, but more so when combined with drug treatments.

Sousa et al. (2007) compared group CBT with the SSRI anti-depressant drug sertraline, finding that group CBT increased complete remission of OCD symptoms more successfully, demonstrating CBT's superiority.

- Trained nurses have proved as effective as psychiatrists and psychologists in treating clients with OCD, demonstrating the simplicity of the treatment and its cost-effectiveness.
- CBT is not suitable for patients who have difficulties talking about inner feelings, or for those who do not possess the verbal skills to do so.

Q   Explain the use of one psychological therapy for the treatment of one anxiety
    disorder.   *(10 marks)*

A Media psychology

1 *Media influences on social behaviour*

Media refers to communication of popular culture, such as television, with a concern as to whether media influence pro- and anti-social behaviour.

▶ Explanations of media influences

Social learning theory. Learning via the media can occur by *indirect reinforcement*, where observed behaviours are reinforced and imitated (*vicarious learning*), enabling humans to learn the value of aggressive behaviour and how and when to imitate specific acts.

Bandura (1965) outlined four steps of modelling:
- *Attention* — attention is paid to attractive, high-status, similar models.
- *Retention* — observed behaviours are memorised.
- *Reproduction* — imitation occurs if individuals have the skills to reproduce observed behaviours.
- *Motivation* — direct and indirect reinforcements, as well as punishments, influence motivation to imitate.

Good levels of *self-efficacy* (situation-specific confidence) are also required.

Research indicates that if observers identify with perpetrators of aggression and/or the more realistic aggression is, the more likely they will be imitated. However, if the perpetrators of aggression are punished, it decreases the chances of imitation.

Bandura et al. (1961, 1963) showed children scenarios involving aggression to a Bobo doll, finding that they were likely to imitate specific behaviours when allowed to play with the doll. Bandura concluded that the chances of aggressive acts being imitated increased if aggressive models were reinforced, but decreased if models were punished, suggesting that imitation only occurs if behaviour is vicariously reinforced. Aggression is more likely to be imitated if children identify with models.

Lovelace and Huston (1983) found that learning from pro-social programmes is situation-specific and that discussion with children after watching such programmes, plus related play, enhances pro-social effects.

- Bobo dolls are not real, cannot retaliate and are designed to be hit. As the situation was unfamiliar, children may have acted as they thought they were supposed to (demand characteristics). There are also ethical concerns over deceit, informed consent, harm and long-term effects on behaviour.
- Many studies measure only short-term effects of pro- and anti-social media and do not differentiate between real aggression and play fighting.

Cognitive priming. The presentation of cues in programmes affects aggressive and pro-social behaviour, people storing violent and pro-social acts that they have seen in their memory as scripts for later behaviour. Being in a similar scenario 'triggers' the script into action.

Murray et al. (2007) took fMRI brain scans of children watching violent and non-violent films, finding that those watching violence had active brain areas associated with emotion and arousal and areas linked to episodic memory. This suggests the storing of aggressive scripts for later use.

- Cognitive priming may affect more those with a disposition for aggression and pro-social behaviour.
- Cognitive priming suggests a practical application in developing pro-social behaviours via media sources.

Stereotyping. Media sources use stereotypes as a quick method of communication. However, these can be non-factual to portray exaggerated models.

> **Dill et al. (2008)** found that men exposed to media stereotypes of sexual harassment became more tolerant of such behaviour. Long-term exposure led to greater tolerance, suggesting that stereotyping has a substantial effect on behaviour.

- Media stereotypes may be so exaggerated as to make imitation of them unsustainable in real-life scenarios.
- Stereotyping may be an effective way of coding pro- and anti-social behaviours in the media.

Desensitisation. Exposure to media violence desensitises and makes people 'comfortably numb' to violence in real life. Desensitisation involves reducing or eliminating cognitive, emotional and behavioural responses to a stimulus.

> **Bushman (2009)** found that participants who played violent video games for 20 minutes took longer to respond to someone injured in a staged fight than those viewing non-violent games, suggesting that desensitisation took place.

- Aretakis and Rameris (2001) believe that over-exposure to media violence retards the development of emotion regulation skills, leading to desensitisation to cues that normally trigger empathetic responding, then leading to aggressive behaviour.

Displacement. Heavy television viewers think the real world more dangerous than it really is. News programmes emphasise this by focusing on violent stories. Showing anti-social behaviours that actually occur less in reality creates a *deviance amplification effect*, where an increasing cycle of reporting of anti-social behaviours occurs.

> **Gerbner and Gross (1976)** found that frequent television viewers rated the real world more dangerous than it is, supporting the idea of displacement.
>
> **Cohen (1968)** reported how an absence of news stories led to a minor affray in Clacton between mods and rockers becoming front-page news, and that this developed into a moral panic, supporting the idea of a deviance amplification effect.

- White (2008) believes that deviance amplification is a media phenomenon that explains the inflated concern with knife crime.

Q Discuss explanations of media influences on pro- and anti-social behaviour.   *(15 marks)*

The effects of video games and computers on young people

Video games. Video games permit more active roles than other media influences, actively encouraging and rewarding violent behaviour within a game. Interest has focused upon whether such behaviour is repeated in real-life scenarios.

Children exposed to video games are retarded in development of emotion regulation skills, leading to desensitisation to cues normally triggering empathetic responding, and increasing the likelihood of violent behaviour.

Desensitisation to violence occurs through repeated exposure to video game aggression, with emotional desensitisation causing a numbing of emotional reactions to events that should produce a response. Cognitive desensitisation occurs when the usual belief that violence is uncommon is

replaced with a belief that violence is commonplace. Desensitisation disrupts the process of moral evaluation, causing action to be taken without consideration of ethical implications.

Individual, gender and age differences occur, as well as a tendency for addictive behaviour. Some research shows game playing to have positive aspects for learning and levels of self-esteem.

Sanger (1996) found that game playing helped develop mastery and control in individuals with low self-esteem, suggesting a positive practical application.

Sopes and Millar (1983) found that children playing video games exhibit addictive tendencies due to the compulsive behavioural involvement; exhibit withdrawal symptoms when attempting to stop playing; and turn to crime to fund their habit.

Kestanbaum and Weinstein (1985) found that game playing helped adolescent males manage developmental conflicts and safely discharge aggression, suggesting that negativity is a parental concern.

Strasburger and Wilson (2002) found that playing video games desensitises users to the consequences of violence, bringing increased pro-violence attitudes and altering cognitive processing. This suggests that video games have negative consequences.

- Evidence from video games research suggests concern, as children's empathy development is retarded and moral evaluation is non-existent, while pro-violence attitudes and behaviour are constantly reinforced.
- Evidence suggests that video games contribute to how individuals construct reality, with an acceptance of violence merged with desensitisation to its consequences.
- Studies have not really focused on the long-term effects of game playing.
- Gee (2003) argues that game playing offers opportunities for experiential learning experiences, especially in developing social and cultural learning and reasoning skills.

Computers. Computers are a growing source of media influence. Interest has focused on relationships lacking face-to-face communication and learning effects. Computers can be a positive tool for communicating, learning and developing social relationships in those lacking social skills and confidence and those living in remote communities, although deception is difficult to detect. There is also the possibility of deindividuation leading to disinhibition, causing individuals to act in non-typical ways.

Caspi and Gorsky (2006) found that one-third of participants used deception, with frequent, younger and more competent users being the main culprits. Those using deception felt it created a sense of harmless enjoyment, suggesting that computer-mediated communication is changing personal moral standards.

Durkin and Barber (2002) found evidence of positive outcomes in adolescents playing computer games. Measures of family closeness, activity involvement, school engagement, mental health, substance misuse and friendship networks were superior in game players than non-players, suggesting that computers are a positive feature of healthy adolescence.

Pearce (2007) presented information to students via printed paper (group A), a film of the printed paper (group B) or displayed on a computer screen (group C). Group A recalled 85% of the information, group B 27%, and group C 4%, suggesting that computers are a poor medium for such learning.

- Research into deception within computer-mediated communication (CMC) is based on online questionnaires, which could be prone to idealised and socially desirable answers, suggesting that findings may not be valid.
- Behrmann (2000) argues that computers can be beneficial if children are encouraged to engage in social interactions and stimulated to acquire knowledge.
- Zhou et al. (2001) found significant cues in CMCs indicating the use of deception and believes that these could be incorporated into an automated tool which would detect deception and protect young people from those with negative intentions.

Q Outline and evaluate the effects of video games and/or computers on young people.

(25 marks)

2 *Persuasion, attitudes and change*

An attitude is a disposition towards an object or situation, prompting individuals to behave in certain ways. Social psychologists became interested in attitude change during the Second World War as mass media became increasingly influential.

Persuasion and attitude change

Hovland–Yale model (1953). Hovland's work centred on the role of persuasion, perceiving attitude change as a response to communication.

Target characteristics relate to the individual receiving and processing communications, less intelligent individuals being seen as more easily persuadable. Self-esteem is important, individuals of moderate levels being more easily persuaded than those of high or low levels. Mood also features as a characteristic.

Source characteristics focus on the credibility of the communicator, more credible communicators being seen as more persuasive, although this may be a short- or long-term effect. Credibility focuses on the expertise, trustworthiness and attractiveness of the communicator.

Message characteristics concentrate on the nature of the communication, presentation of both sides of an argument being seen as more persuasive towards attitude change.

Overall attitude change is perceived as a sequential process, comprising stages of *attention* (the target attends to the message), *comprehension* (the target understands the message), *reactance* (the target reacts to the message either positively or negatively) and *acceptance* (the message is accepted if perceived as credible).

Meveritz and Chaiken (1987) discovered that scary messages were more persuasive towards attitude change, suggesting that fear plays a role. However, extremely scary messages caused people to ignore them.

Allyn and Festinger (1961) found that distracting people made them more persuadable than capturing their full attention, suggesting a strategy to achieve attitude change.

Walster and Festinger (1962) found that deliberately targeted messages were less persuasive.

- The model describes the process of attitude change, rather than explaining it.
- Research tends to be laboratory based, showing causality and allowing for replication. However, due to the artificial environment, findings may not be truly valid.
- Research exploring the role of fear in persuasive messages can be seen as harmful and therefore unethical.

Elaboration likelihood model (Petty and Cacioppo 1986). This model explains how persuasive messages are processed, perceiving two forms of cognitive routes by which persuasive attitude change occurs through cognitive evaluation.
- The *central route* occurs when individuals are presented with material and are motivated to analyse it and reach an attitude-changing conclusion. This route is used for messages requiring elaborated cognitive effort. These need to be robust, as persuasion is influenced by the quality of the message. If favourable thoughts are produced, attitude change is likely.
- The *peripheral route* occurs when individuals are motivated to consider the source of a communication to change an attitude, rather than the message itself. This route only considers superficial cues, such as the perceived credibility of the communicator and the quality of the presentation, with the logic behind a message seen as irrelevant and no elaboration required.

As motivation and the ability to process a message increase, it becomes more likely that the central route will be used, although with moderate elaboration, a mixture of central and peripheral routes are used. Motivational factors include personal relevance of the message, accountability and an individual's innate desire to indulge in thinking. Ability factors include the availability of cognitive resources, such as distractions, and relevant knowledge necessary to analyse arguments.

> **Miller (2005)** found that peripheral route processing relies on environmental conditions, such as the perceived credibility of the source, the quality of its presentation, the attractiveness of the source and catchy slogans. This offers support to the model.
>
> **Petty et al. (1981)** found students influenced by persuasive messages when they were personally motivated and by peripheral cues when not personally motivated.

- Although the model has explanatory power, it lacks predictive ability in different contexts.
- Chaiken (1980) proposes a *heuristic-systematic model* using two processing modes. Communications can be attended to either carefully by *analytical systematic processing*, or by the use of *heuristic mental shortcuts*, such as using stereotypes to make decisions. This alternative model permits a wider range of specific predictions.

Q Compare the Hovland–Yale and elaboration likelihood models of persuasion and attitude change. *(25 marks)*

The influence of attitudes on decision making

Cognitive consistency sees humans as motivated to process information to reach mental equilibrium (balance). However, humans often experience two inconsistent attitudes, and cognitive dissonance theory attempts to explain how such occurrences are dealt with.

Cognitive dissonance (Festinger 1957). Dissonance is a negative state experienced when two cognitions (pieces of knowledge) are inconsistent with each other, creating motivation to return to a more balanced state. Often cognitions are related and link together logically (consonant): for example, having a 'sweet tooth' and liking chocolate. However, sometimes they are related, but are not logically linked (dissonant): for example, liking chocolate and wishing to lose weight.

Dissonance can be addressed in several ways, such as ignoring it (e.g. pretending chocolate is not fattening), lowering its importance (e.g. believing that losing weight is not vital), adding in new cognitions (e.g. doing a lot of exercise), or preventing dissonance occurring at all (e.g. avoiding information about chocolate).

The model explains how dissonance occurs after decisions are made, by providing support for the chosen option and focusing on the negative aspects of the unchosen option.

> **Festinger and Carlsmith (1959)** paid participants either $1 or $20 to perform a boring task, finding that those paid a small amount said the task was more interesting than those paid a lot. They had unconsciously rated the task more interesting because they experienced dissonance through having no financial incentive to say so, and were motivated to reduce the dissonance.
>
> **Knox and Inkster (1968)** found that people betting on horses became more confident their horse would win after placing a bet, showing how dissonance occurs after decisions are made.

- Deaux (1995) believes that dissonance provides the best explanation of post-decisional attitude change and that the concept is flexible, being applicable to most decision-making situations.
- One problem with cognitive consistency/dissonance is that it does not explain why attitudes should be consistent.

Self-perception theory (Bem 1972). This model does not believe that people experience the negative state drive of dissonance, perceiving instead that individuals come to know their attitudes, emotions and internal states, inferring them from observing their own behaviour and the circumstances in which they occur. The model has a different view of how attitudes influence decision making,

believing that if an individual does something for a big reward, then behaviour is attributed to the reward, with motivation to perform well being perceived as low. However, if something is done for a small reward, then behaviour is seen as due to internal attributions, such as task enjoyment, with motivation to perform well being higher. Therefore, if behaviour is seen as externally caused, it is perceived as not matching true internal feelings, a phenomenon known as the *overjustification effect.*

Deci (1972) reported on a man who, plagued by boys kicking a ball against his wall, promised them a financial reward to continue their behaviour. On subsequent days he continually reduced the amount of the reward, until the boys refused to carry on, lending support to the idea that external rewards reduce intrinsic motivation.

Guild et al. (2006) found significant attitude changes in psychology students who had to write a statement arguing against an issue towards which they had previously held a positive attitude, supporting self-perception theory rather than dissonance theory.

- Both cognitive dissonance and self-perception theories may be correct, but in different situations. Social perception theory seems best in situations where attitudes and behaviour do not fit, but strong attitudes are not held, while cognitive dissonance theory works best in situations where there is a large gap between behaviour and attitudes.

Q Outline and evaluate the influence of attitudes on decision making. *(20 marks)*

Explanations for the effectiveness of television in persuasion

The Hovland–Yale and elaboration likelihood models of attitude change can both be used as explanations for the effectiveness of television in persuasion.

Hovland–Yale model. Three factors can be used to explain the effectiveness of television in persuasion:
- *Communicator.* Television uses skilled communicators possessing attractive qualities and excellent communicative abilities. Constant exposure increases their persuasiveness as we identify with and look up to them.
- *Message.* The means by which messages are communicated is a strong factor, television being influential due to its immediacy, availability and numerous formats. The persuasiveness of television works best for simple messages, with alternative means, such as written media, better for complex ones.
- *Audience.* Males are more persuadable by female-based topics and females more persuadable by male-based topics. Research also indicates age-related differences.

Sistrunk and McDavid (1971) found female-orientated television topics more persuasive on male attitudes than female ones, suggesting a gender difference in the persuasiveness of television.

Hugo-Saylor et al. (1992) found that pre-schoolers' themes of play were 'hurricane based' following television coverage of a hurricane, suggesting that receiver response characteristics are age dependent.

- Producing attitude change by using communicators with positive qualities and similarities to the audience can also be explained in terms of social learning theory, where the audience observes and imitates the communicator as a form of vicarious reinforcement.

Elaboration likelihood model. Effective persuasion comes from using the central route, where an individual is motivated to analyse material carefully. Messages have to be robust and personally important, requiring elaborated cognitive effort. The use of strong arguments when presenting material, encouraging people to analyse and think about points being made and cutting out possible distractions, also helps to achieve this.

The peripheral route, where the source of the communication rather than the message itself is considered, has a role in the effectiveness of television persuasiveness, with people in contented moods more likely to use this route, as they wish to maintain their positive emotive state.

Audiences must have their attention captured and this occurs by the use of heightened emotions, such as fear, although too much fear puts people on the defensive and makes them unwilling to elaborate cognitive processing.

> **Witte and Allen (2000)** found that messages containing strong fear and high efficacy content produce the greatest change in attitudes in anti-smoking campaigns.
>
> **Gorn and Goldberg (1980)** found moderate message repetition effective, as it presents opportunities for elaborated scrutiny. However, over-usage was ineffective, as it produces tedium.

- Television usage of psychological models and methods to achieve attitude change may be unethical as people are being manipulated without informed consent: that is, they are being influenced by propaganda rather than education.
- The use of psychological models and methods as persuasive elements is important in programmes involving debates, campaigns and viewer participation.

Q Discuss explanations for the effectiveness of television in persuasion. *(25 marks)*

3 The psychology of celebrity

Celebrities are widely recognised individuals with high public profiles. Obsession with celebrity is found in all forms of media, arousing considerable debate about its influence upon society and upon specific groups such as children, with modern phenomena such as stalking arousing concern. Various theories have been offered as explanations, including social psychological and evolutionary ones.

Social psychological explanations for the attraction of celebrity

Social learning theory. Celebrities in the media have qualities causing us to identify with them as role models, so we imitate them due to vicarious reinforcement.

Social identity theory. Collective admiration of celebrities and membership of fan clubs etc. creates in-group and out-group membership as part of an individual's social identity.

Social construction theory. Celebrity is perceived as a self-serving, social invention of the media, providing continual interest and focus (maintenance), which generates income.

Absorption–addiction model. Individuals develop interest in celebrities due to a lack of meaningful relationships in their lives and as an attempt to escape mundane reality. In stronger forms, the interest in celebrity becomes addictive, individuals feeling a need for more involvement with celebrities, correlating strongly with diminished psychological health.

Positive–active model. Interest in celebrities is seen in a positive light, entailing involvement in active participation, such as participating in social networks (e.g. fan clubs) that can enhance social skills.

> **Escalis and Bettman (2008)** found that celebrity endorsement enhances products when consumers aspire to be like the celebrity, supporting social psychological explanations, especially social learning theory.
>
> **Belch and Belch (2007)** found that celebrities are often well liked, leading to identification in an attempt to seek a kind of relationship with the celebrity, supporting the absorption–addiction model.

- The fact that 20% of advertisements in the USA feature celebrities suggests a social learning effect.
- Crocker and Park (2004) believe that people have an interest in celebrities as they are motivated to have a favourable self-identity and by a need to maintain and enhance self-esteem.
- The majority of research into the attraction of celebrity has been done in Western cultures and so findings may be culturally specific.

Evolutionary explanations for the attraction of celebrity

The attractiveness of celebrity is seen as serving an adaptive function.

Gossip. Dunbar (1997) believes that groups grew so large that gossip became an effective manner of communicating information about social relationships and hierarchies, explaining the appeal of celebrity journalism as communicating observations about alpha males and females.

Attractiveness. Evolutionary theory sees attractiveness as adaptive, incurring better reproduction opportunities. Interest in celebrities focuses on their enhanced attractiveness, explaining their lofty status.

Gender. Interest in celebrity is more female orientated because females compare males as a means of selection. Interest in female celebrities occurs as females compete in levels of attractiveness and learn attractiveness skills from alpha females.

Prestige hypothesis. Individuals benefit from imitating prestigious people, such imitation bringing more resources, protection and reproductive opportunities.

Dunbar (1997) reports that two-thirds of conversation is spent on social topics, supporting the idea that language evolved for social purposes.

Fieldman (2008) found that females find male celebrities attractive because of qualities advertising toughness, stamina and high levels of testosterone, all indicators of good genetic quality and an ability to provide resources.

- Celebrity journalism often focuses on attractiveness, romantic liaisons and reproductive success, supporting the idea that attraction to celebrity has an evolutionary basis.
- Reynolds (2009) believes that evolution programs us to find certain individuals attractive because we share similar genes and have the same perception of beauty, suggesting a reason why celebrities are universally popular.

Q Evaluate explanations of the attraction of celebrity. *(10 marks)*

Research into intense fandom

Some individuals form such an interest in celebrities that they become parasocial (one-sided) relationships. Such intense fandom occurs at several levels, from a fairly harmless, even healthy, form of celebrity worship, to more sinister levels, such as stalking, defined as 'the wilful, malicious and repeated following or harassing of another person that threatens his or her safety'.

TOPIC 10 | Psychology in action

Celebrity

McCutcheon et al. (2002) developed the Celebrity Attitude Scale, measuring items on three categories of celebrity worship:

- *Entertainment sub-scale* — social aspects of celebrity worship, such as discussions with friends.
- *Intense personal sub-scale* — strength of feelings and levels of obsession.
- *Borderline pathological sub-scale* — levels of uncontrollable feelings and behaviour.

Celebrity worship was found to have a single dimension, with lower-scoring individuals showing an avid interest in celebrities, such as reading about them, while high-scoring individuals tend to over-identify and become obsessive about celebrities

Maltby et al. (2003) found three dimensions of fandom:

- *Entertainment social* — people attracted to celebrities for their entertainment value.
- *Intense personal* — people who develop obsessive tendencies towards celebrities.
- *Borderline pathological* — people who develop uncontrollable fantasies and behaviour patterns.

Maltby et al. (2004) found that those in the entertainment-social category were mentally healthy, but those in higher categories were prone to poor mental and physical health.

McCutcheon and Houran (2003) found that a third of people suffer from celebrity worship syndrome, a fascination with the lives of the famous; 20% followed celebrities in the media for entertainment-social reasons; 10% develop an intense personal attitude towards celebrities; 1% of participants were classed as borderline pathological, exhibiting impulsive, anti-social behaviour indicative of psychosis. This suggests that celebrity worship does not make someone dysfunctional, but increases the chances of their being so.

- Mild forms of celebrity worship can be beneficial. Larsen (1995) found that intense attachments to celebrities provided young people with attitudinal and behavioural exemplars.
- West and Sweeting (2002) recommend media training in schools, illustrating the dangers of celebrity worship and eating disorders, especially in adolescent girls.

Stalking

Mullen (2008) scrutinised 20,000 incidents of stalking the royal family, finding that 80% were by persons with psychotic disorders, such as schizophrenia, which is very different from people who stalk non-famous people, suggesting that celebrity stalking is a separate phenomenon.

Purcell et al. (2002) found a tendency for criminal activity and drug abuse in male stalkers and they had a range of reasons for stalking, whereas females tended to be of a nurturing disposition, stalked people they knew and were searching for intimacy. This suggests a gender difference in stalking behaviour.

Kamphuis and Emmelkamp (2000) found that 25% of stalking cases culminate in violence, 2% leading to murder. However, there are variations, such as: the erotomanic stalker, usually female, with a delusional belief that an older man of status is in love with her; obsessional stalkers, who stalk after a relationship has gone sour; resentful stalkers, who stalk to frighten; predatory stalkers, who precipitate sexual attacks; and psychotic stalkers, who target famous people. This suggests that the general label of 'stalker' is too wide, there appearing to be several types of stalker with different profiles, who indulge in stalking for different reasons.

McCutcheon et al. (2006) found that individuals with insecure attachment types had positive attitudes towards stalking and those with pathological attachment types had a tendency to stalk, suggesting that stalking behaviour is linked to childhood attachment patterns.

- Research into stalking may create an understanding of the behaviour, leading to the formation of effective treatments.
- Research into stalking is problematic, as definitions vary from country to country, making estimates of its frequency difficult.
- Obsessive, rejected stalkers have responded favourably to psychotherapy, but psychopathic stalkers who prey on celebrities have proved resistant to treatment, indicating that different forms of stalking may be separate from each other.

- Legal intervention, such as trespassing orders, is the best way of dealing with celebrity stalkers, but this can stimulate stalkers into even more malicious behaviour.

Q Discuss research into intense fandom. *(25 marks)*

B The psychology of addictive behaviour

1 *Models of addictive behaviour*

Biological, cognitive and learning models

Biological model of addiction. The biological model perceives addiction as a physiologically controlled pattern of behaviour. The initiation of addiction is seen as occurring by genetic vulnerability, while maintenance of addiction occurs through activation of dopamine, which some drugs, such as cocaine, have a direct effect upon. Relapse is due to physiological cravings.

Drugs affect the nervous system, especially synapses, by reducing or increasing the frequency of nerve impulses. They can block neurotransmitter receptor sites, or attach to receptors and have the same effect as a neurotransmitter — preventing neurotransmitters from recycling, so that they remain in the synapse and reattach to receptor sites.

> **Overstreet et al. (1993)** found that different genetic strains of rats demonstrated differences in levels of liking for alcohol, suggesting that preference for alcohol is under genetic control.
>
> **Nielsen et al. (2008)** compared DNA from former heroin addicts and non-addicts, finding a relationship between addiction and certain gene variants. Some genes also act against becoming addicted, indicating a genetic basis to addiction.

- The model relies on evidence from animal studies, which may not be generalisable to humans.
- Biological explanations are incomplete, not considering the important role that psychological factors play.
- Addiction to one drug can produce cross-tolerance of other related drugs, such as opiates. In addition, withdrawal symptoms after abstaining from one drug can be addressed by taking a similar drug, such as methadone for heroin. This suggests that similar drugs act upon the nervous system in the same way, supporting the biological model.

Cognitive model of addiction. Addiction is seen as due to distorted thinking relating to dysfunctional beliefs about drug use, such as intellectual functioning being dependent on drug use. These maladaptive cognitive processes may relate to mood, causing addicts to believe that happiness is impossible without the drug. Dysfunctional beliefs are self-fulfilling, leading to a perception of personal incapability in controlling drug usage, and forming an inability to direct attention away from addictive behaviour.

Faulty thinking leads addicts to focus on positive features of drug use and to minimise negative ones, again strengthening dependency. Another cognitive feature is impaired decision-making abilities, with addicts focusing on strategies of immediate pleasure, even knowing that such choices are harmful in the long term.

The model therefore sees initiation, maintenance and relapses as due to maladaptive thought processes.

Koski-Jannes (1992) found that addictions form from short-sighted means of dealing with stressful situations, giving initially positive, but later negative consequences, leading to a self-perpetuating cycle of addiction regulated by self-serving thoughts. This suggests that the cognitive model can explain how addictions are initiated.

Ratelle et al. (2004) found that gambling addicts had persistent thoughts about gambling and poorer concentration on daily tasks, indicating a cognitive element to addiction.

- The biological model is a better explanation of the initiation of dependency, but the cognitive model more ably accounts for maintenance and relapses.
- Cognitive models offer incomplete explanations, being based upon expectations and beliefs, thus ignoring important biological factors.
- The relative success of cognitive-behavioural treatments suggests that addiction must have a cognitive component.

Learning models of addiction. Addictive behaviour is explained by classical conditioning, operant conditioning and social learning theory. With classical conditioning, drug use becomes associated with environmental factors until those factors alone produce a 'high'. Operant conditioning sees addiction arising from positive reinforcements, such as euphoric drug 'highs', and negative reinforcements, such as reductions in anxiety, serving to strengthen addictive behaviours by increasing the chances of recurrence, with increased drug usage perceived as an attempt to increase these reinforcements. The neurotransmitter dopamine is identified as a reinforcer within the brain reward system, many drugs acting upon dopamine synapses to produce euphoria.

Social learning theory sees addiction as resulting from vicarious learning, dependent behaviour being observed and imitated if incurring the model as reinforcement.

Meyer et al. (1995) found that the sight of hypodermic needles created positive feelings in addicts, demonstrating the role of classical conditioning in addictive behaviour.

Farber et al. (1980) found an important difference between alcohol use through negative reinforcement (escape drinking) and positive reinforcement (social drinking), suggesting that specific learning factors are linked to addiction.

Bahr et al. (2005) found that drug taking by peers was a big influence in initiating drug use, suggesting a role for social learning theory.

- The fact many abstaining addicts do not experience withdrawal symptoms and cravings suggests that biological factors are not as important as learning ones.
- Many forms of addiction respond favourably to behavioural treatments, indicating a learning component. However, such treatments often produce only short-term benefits, suggesting that symptoms are being addressed, but not causes, implying that others factors must be involved too.

Q (a) Outline the cognitive model of addiction.   *(9 marks)*
   (b) Evaluate the biological model of addiction.   *(16 marks)*

Explanations for specific addictions

Smoking

Smoking produces a physical addiction to nicotine, influencing dopamine production and the brain reward system.

Biological explanations. Nicotine affects the production of dopamine and acetylcholine, leading to a reinforcing effect. Genetic variations indicate that some people are more vulnerable to dependency.

Operant conditioning. Maintenance of smoking is due to the positive reinforcement that nicotine inhalation produces. As nicotine is removed from the body, frequent reinforcements via smoking are required.

Social learning theory. Smoking occurs via observation and imitation of role models, due to vicarious reinforcement.

Cognitive explanations. Smokers possess irrational thoughts, such dysfunctional ideas being self-fulfilling, creating the belief that they cannot quit, and leading to a 'vicious circle' of continually giving in to cravings.

> **Pergadia et al. (2006)** found a heritability factor in the experience of nicotine withdrawal symptoms, suggesting a genetic link and supporting biological explanations.
>
> **Goldberg et al. (1981)** found that monkeys will press a lever in a Skinner box to receive nicotine at a similar rate to that for cocaine, suggesting that smoking is maintained through its reinforcing effect. This supports operant conditioning as an explanation.
>
> **National Institute on Drug Abuse (2005)** found that 90% of smokers started as adolescents, due to observation and imitation of peers, suggesting that initiation of smoking is due to social learning theory.

- The fact that biological therapies help people quit supports the biological explanation.
- Many quit without nicotine replacement or cravings, suggesting a role for social and cognitive factors.
- Addiction seems to be mainly psychological, there seeming to be little change in nicotine receptors that would characterise biological tolerance.

Gambling

Gambling does not involve dependency on a substance, but its symptoms and effects are the same as for drug addiction.

Personality. Research indicates that gamblers are impulsive, high sensation seekers and susceptible to boredom. Other characteristics are sensitivity to punishment and reward-orientation; qualities that make gambling successes have a strong positive effect, explaining continuation into dependency.

Cognitive explanations. Irrational thought patterns distort beliefs about skill levels and luck, successes being perceived as due to skill and losing due to luck or not paying attention. Superstitious beliefs develop to account for winning and losing, leading to greater risk taking and increased persistence.

Biological explanations. Gambling increases dopamine production, creating pleasurable sensations in the brain reward system. Research indicates that genetic factors are involved, with some at risk of developing multiple addictions. Genetics can explain why some are more at risk of addiction, as genetics may bestow different levels of dependency vulnerability.

> **Loxton et al. (2008)** found that chronic gamblers score higher on impulsiveness and reward-orientation than non-gamblers, suggesting that dependency is connected to personality.
>
> **Griffiths (1994)** found that habitual users of fruit machines tended to hold irrational beliefs about losing, such as not concentrating, and attributed successes to personal skill, suggesting a cognitive explanation.
>
> **Grosset et al. (2009)** found that dopamine agonists used to treat Parkinson's disease turned 10% of patients into pathological gamblers, suggesting that dopamine is linked to gambling dependency, which supports the biological explanation.

- The fact that dopamine is linked to dependency may lead to the manufacture of drugs acting upon dopamine production, which could reduce gambling dependency and other forms of addiction too.

- Paul (2008) reports that 20% of teenage gambling addicts contemplate suicide, demonstrating the need for explanations of the condition, in order to develop effective treatments.
- Care must be taken when conducting research with dependent gamblers — indeed any kind of addict — as ethical concerns of harm are heightened and it is arguable whether people with such pathological conditions can give informed consent.

Q Outline and evaluate explanations of gambling addiction. *(25 marks)*

2 *Factors affecting addictive behaviour*

Vulnerability to addiction

Several factors affect vulnerability to addiction: that is, each person's level of risk of becoming addicted. These can be applied to all forms of dependent behaviour.

Self-esteem. This refers to levels of self-worth and is part of our self-concept, closely linked to confidence and motivational levels. Low levels of self-esteem are associated with developing dependency and depression. As low self-esteem can result from falling short of our ideal self, it may be that individuals with low self-esteem are more vulnerable to dependency in order to escape reality.

Fieldman et al. (1995) compared heroin and cocaine addicts on personality factors, finding personality in drug addicts associated with lower self-esteem and negative self-evaluation.

Gonzalez (2003) found 15% of Spanish teenagers at risk of becoming addicted to mobile phone use, seeing the behaviour as an obsessive-compulsive problem linked to low self-esteem, with persistent phone usage an attempt to develop confidence.

- Although research indicates that people with low levels of self-esteem are vulnerable to addiction, this may not be a causal relationship, as being addicted may lead to lower self-esteem.
- Psychological therapies based upon raising self-esteem levels in addicts may be successful in helping people to quit and not relapse.

Attributions for addiction. Attributions concern explanations that individuals give for their own and others' behaviour. This involves the *fundamental attribution error*, where a person perceives their behaviour as due to *situational* attributions (externally controlled), with other people's behaviour as due to *dispositional* attributions (internally controlled). Addicts see their dependency as due to external, situational factors (e.g. 'I have to take drugs to get respect'). However, they see other addicts' behaviour as due to internal, dispositional (personality) factors (e.g. 'She's an addict because she has no self-respect'). Attribution theory explains why addicts relapse when attempting to quit — because they explain attributions as due to external factors, such as high stress levels, which are perceived as beyond their control.

Seneviratne and Saunders (2000) found that alcoholics saw the relapses of others as due to an internal locus of causality (e.g. having poor willpower), while their own relapses were seen as due to an external locus of control (i.e. factors beyond their control and therefore not their fault).

Bradley et al. (1992) found that addicts who attributed more responsibility for negative outcomes and relapse episodes to personally controllable factors were more likely to quit using opiates, suggesting that attribution theory can explain vulnerability to dependency.

- Attribution theory adds to our understanding of addictions by providing information about the cognitive mechanisms and processes by which situations and personal vulnerabilities influence behaviour.

- Support for attribution theory comes from the fact that successful quitters in clinics relapse outside the clinic, as they attribute quitting to the external situation (the clinic).

Social context of addiction. Social contexts influence vulnerability to dependency in several ways. Parents and peers can be an influence through their norms towards addictive behaviours and by the degree of social support provided to those attempting to quit. Being involved in social contexts that encourage one form of addiction can act as a 'gateway' to trying other forms of addiction. Environmental factors are important, with homeless people and those in poor housing being at risk, as are factors associated with social status — single people and divorcees having been identified as more vulnerable. Changing attitudes also influence risk of dependency, such as an increase in female smoking. Social contexts also influence vulnerability by acting as cues, such as an abstinent drinker getting cravings in a pub setting.

Sproull and Keisler (1998) found that reducing social context cues helped to alleviate addiction, indicating that such cues increase risk of dependency.

Kendler et al. (2000) found that as attitudes towards women smoking became less negative, more women smoked, suggesting that changes in social attitudes affect vulnerability levels.

Stein et al. (2008) found the homeless and those in poor housing to be highly vulnerable to dependency.

- Leshner (1998) believes that treatments must include social context elements if they are to be successful, as recovered addicts may relapse when leaving a clinic, due to the original social context still being in place.
- Social context effects are complex, consisting of several factors, all of which must be considered if accurate levels of vulnerability are to be assessed.

Q Discuss factors that affect vulnerability to addiction. *(25 marks)*

The role of the media in addictive behaviour

Research has examined the extent to which the media affect addictive behaviours. The many forms of media have varying influences on different age groups, the focus mainly being on social learning effects of various media, many of which are seen as presenting enhanced opportunities towards dependency behaviours. Another aspect is that of addiction to media themselves, creating a physiological dependence on social media and user-generated content, with research indicating it to be a growing problem, due to the ever-increasing provision of media formats into people's lives, such as the internet and expanding television channels. The media, through their content, can also affect people's conceptions of addiction risks, often in an invalid manner.

Gunsekera et al. (2005) found drug taking in films to be portrayed in a positive fashion with little reference to negative consequences, suggesting that the media can influence dependency behaviour.

Kimberley (2006) found social media to be addictive in themselves, leading to increased usage to sustain 'highs' and increased anxiety without periodic access. Even minor exposure creates physical and psychological dependence, suggesting social media addiction (SMA) to be a real and troublesome condition.

Walther (1999) reported on the increase in communication addiction disorder, where the disinhibition of the internet makes it attractive to potential addicts who have problems in establishing and maintaining normal social relationships, creating disturbances in psychosocial functioning and an individual's ability to maintain positive work practices.

- Media sources have proved influential with children, who tend not to question their credibility, suggesting that there should be an embargo on the broadcast of programmes with content pertaining to addictive practices until after children's bedtime.

TOPIC 10   Psychology in action

- The Centre for Addiction Recovery has developed the Internet Addiction Test so that people can assess if they are at risk of developing SMA, demonstrating how psychology can be used in a practical manner.
- Farber (2007) reports that SMA is an increasing problem at work, many employees feeling a constant need to access social media sites to the point of addiction, suggesting that such behaviour seriously affects performance.
- There is a danger that addicts can be demonised through media-created moral panics, seriously affecting the chances of addicts receiving adequate social support to help them abstain, or even of seeking treatment in the first place.

Q   Outline the role of the media in addictive behaviour.   *(9 marks)*

3   *Reducing addictive behaviour*

Models of prevention

Theory of reasoned action (TRA) (Ajzen and Fishbein 1980). The model views addictive behaviours and attempts to control or abstain from them as due to decision making and the factors underpinning such decision making, rather than being the result of predisposing factors. The model includes the component of behavioural intention in the process of persuasion and is explicitly concerned with behaviour, although recognising the role of attitudes in behaviour. Because behavioural intention is separated from actual behaviour, the model is able to examine factors limiting the effects of behavioural intentions on actual behaviour, using the elements of attitudes and the expectation of others to predict behavioural intent.

Behavioural intent is due to two factors, *attitudes* and *subjective norms*. Attitudes are perceived as having two components, *evaluation* and *strength* of a belief. Subjective norms also have two components: *normative beliefs* (what a person believes others expect of them) and *motivation to comply* (how important it is to do what others expect).

TRA explains why addictions continue and why some can abstain, some find it impossible, and some can, but relapse. If an individual's attitudes and normative beliefs support abstention, their behavioural intention will be to quit and this will need a *belief* about the effects of addictive behaviour and abstaining from it, an *evaluation* that the consequences will be positive, an *expectation* of others that this will be worthwhile and *personal motivation* to satisfy expectations. Each of these provides reasons to continue usage or to relapse — but, positively, suggests a means of abstaining.

Crano et al. (2008) used TRA to estimate adolescents' vulnerability to inhalant abuse, by assessing intentions to use or avoid inhalants and actual behaviour. The model was accurate as a predictive tool and thus useful in helping addicts to abstain.

Wood and Griffith (2004) assessed adolescents' gambling behaviour, finding attitudes a good predictor of actual behaviour, supporting TRA..

DeFleur and Westie (1958) found evidence that the model's assumption of a direct link between thinking and behaviour is wrong, casting doubt upon its usefulness.

Laflin (1994) found, consistent with TRA, that drug attitudes and subjective norms were more useful in predicting drug and alcohol consumption than levels of self-esteem, demonstrating the usefulness of the model.

- Critics see TRA as deficient in explaining the behaviour of those who have, or perceive, little control over their behaviour, with this applying strongly to addicts.
- TRA predicts behavioural intention and behaviour, but cannot necessarily explain behavioural change, which is the primary concern in dependency education programmes.

- TRA does not consider personality and cultural factors, or demographic variables that shape behaviour, limiting its use as a model of prevention.
- Addicts are often aware that their behaviour is irrational, such as heavy drinkers wanting to abstain, but even when intentions, attitudes and norms indicate that they will, many still do not. This suggests that dependent behaviour may not be reasoned, weakening the impact of the model.

Theory of planned behaviour (TPB) (Ajzen 1988). TRA was modified to produce TPB, adding a new component, the influence of perceived control. The model has several components.

Behavioural beliefs link the behaviour of interest to expected outcomes and comprise the subjective probability that behaviour would produce a given response. Behavioural beliefs determine the prevailing *attitude towards a behaviour* — the degree to which performance of such behaviour is positively or negatively valued.

Normative beliefs refer to perceived behavioural expectations of the relevant social group, combining with levels of motivation to determine prevailing *subjective norms* — the perceived social pressure to be involved or not in the behaviour.

Control beliefs involve the perceived presence of factors that help or hinder performance of behaviour, and they are seen as determining *perceived behavioural control* — people's beliefs about their ability to perform a given behaviour. To the degree that it is an accurate measurement of behavioural control, perceived behavioural control can, along with *intention*, be used to predict behaviour, intention being a measure of an individual's willingness to perform a behaviour.

TPB considers an individual's reasons for continuing with dependency behaviours and their personal belief in their resolve to abstain, these being important in resolving to abstain and in resisting withdrawal effects and cravings. To succeed, a person's perceived behavioural control must be able to lead them to believe they can overcome problems: for example, an alcoholic must be convinced that they will not buy alcohol, go to pubs, or accept drinks from others. The more a person believes they have behavioural control, the more the model predicts success in abstaining, and the harder abstention is perceived to be, the more persistent they will be in attempting to quit.

Walker et al. (2006) assessed whether TSB explains gambling behaviour. Although some attitudes and norms were important, controllability was not an important factor for many participants in determining intention. Intention was found to be an important predictive factor, indicating some support for the model.

Oh and Hsu (2001) assessed gamblers' previous gambling behaviour, their social norms, attitudes, perceived behavioural control (e.g. perceived gambling skills) and levels of self-control, along with their behavioural intentions. A relationship was found between attitudes, behavioural intentions and actual behaviour, supporting the model.

- The model assumes that behaviours are conscious, reasoned and planned, which may not always be the case with addicts.
- As with TRA, TRB may be reliant on invalid evidence, as research tends to rely on self-reports, which may be subject to social desirability, such as addicts playing down their degree of dependency, or even not being aware of the true extent of their dependency.
- Although contributing to an understanding of addiction, the lack of universal research support suggests that further explanations are required if prevention treatments are to increase their successfulness.

Q Outline and evaluate one model of prevention associated with reducing addictive behaviour.

(25 marks)

Types of intervention

Biological interventions

Detoxification programmes. These involve gradual or instant abstention, using antagonistic drugs, which block neurotransmitter receptors so that synaptic transmission is prevented, thus reducing withdrawal effects. Alternatively, drugs can be used to address dependency directly.

Drug maintenance therapy. This involves using substitute drugs, such as methadone for heroin addicts. Methadone produces less of a high, is taken orally and does not involve contextual cues, such as needles. Antagonistic and agonistic drugs can be used.
- *Antagonistic drugs* lessen or eliminate the effects of neurotransmitters by blocking cellular activity, altering the effects of addictive drugs.
- *Agonistic drugs* are site-specific drugs triggering cellular activity. As many drugs act upon dopamine levels to produce a 'high', dopamine agonists are used, also lessening withdrawal symptoms by producing more dopamine in the brain.

Nicotine replacement therapy. Although nicotine is addictive, it is other components of cigarettes, such as tar, which are dangerous. In nicotine replacement therapy, nicotine is imbibed by means other than smoking, such as patches or gum.

Moore et al. (2009) found nicotine replacement therapies to be effective in achieving sustained abstinence for smokers who cannot or will not attempt immediate abstinence.

Warren et al. (2005) assessed the effectiveness of methadone as a treatment for heroin addiction among prisoners. Inmates receiving methadone used heroin on an average of 15.24 days a year compared to 99.96 days a year for inmates not receiving methadone, showing methadone to be extremely effective.

- Drugs can have side-effects. Varenicline, used to treat smoking dependency, can result in depression and suicide, although withdrawal symptoms may contribute too.
- Methadone, an antagonist used to treat heroin addiction, is associated with psychiatric disorders such as depression. Trauer (2008) found those on methadone maintenance ten times more likely to have psychiatric disorders than the general population.

Psychological interventions

Cognitive therapies. These forge trusting relationships, taking an active, focused approach to identify and deconstruct false beliefs, reduce craving and help establish control over addictive behaviours. Triggers are identified and strategies developed that increase willpower, so that self-control becomes greater than the strength of the craving. Increased control is developed in therapy, by artificially creating situations producing cravings and developing methods of resistance, such as rational explanations, to address false beliefs.

Cognitive-behavioural therapy affects how addicts think about dependency. Behavioural self-control training, enabling an addict to realise when they are at risk, is combined with coping skills, such as relaxation techniques, to help resist temptation.

Aversion therapy. This is a behaviourist treatment based on classical conditioning, where a negative effect is paired with the addictive substance so that the two become associated together.

Operant conditioning. This is behaviourist treatment based on voluntary behaviours. Reinforcement, such as being allowed visits, is experienced when an addict stays drug free for a target period. Token economies utilise operant conditioning and are used in therapeutic communities, where non-addictive behaviour is rewarded with tokens that can be exchanged for desirable goods.

Higgins et al. (1994) found that 75% of cocaine addicts using token economies completed a drug rehabilitation course, compared to 40% using psychotherapy.

Carroll et al. (2008) found that addicts assigned to CBT produced more negative urine samples and longer periods of abstinence, suggesting that CBT is an effective method of treating substance abuse.

- Behavioural treatments often have short-term, but not long-term, success in addressing addictions, possibly because they are addressing the effects of dependency rather than causes.
- CBT can be tailored to many individuals' circumstances and situations. Its effects are long-lasting and can address the dependencies of the severely addicted.

Public health interventions

Legislation and policing. Making drugs illegal prevents some usage, but can increase criminality.

Bans on smoking indoors have led to an increase in smoking outdoors and attempts to ban gambling and drinking drove such activities underground, again heightening criminal activity.

Health promotion. This occurs in many ways with varying degrees of success.
- *Fear arousal* is often used in health campaigns to strengthen the persuasiveness of arguments against addictive practices.
- *Targeting risk groups* is based on the idea that health promotion campaigns are successful if they are specifically orientated towards those at risk.

Quist-Paulsen and Gallefoss (2007) found that fear arousal reduced smoking in cardiac patients, suggesting that such a strategy is effective.

Conrod et al. (2004) found that targeting resources at adolescents at risk of developing substance abuse incurred successful outcomes.

- Smoking bans reduce cigarette sales, but make chronic smokers more determined not to quit.
- It is difficult to evaluate legislative attempts to curb addictive practices, as criminalisation makes it difficult to assess how many users there are.
- Identifying risk groups can be cost-effective, as it targets resources at those who benefit most from them.

Q Outline and evaluate types of intervention that can reduce addictive behaviour. *(20 marks)*

C Anomalistic psychology

1 *Theoretical and methodological issues*

Issues of pseudoscience and scientific fraud

Pseudoscience means 'false science' and refers to so-called sciences and scientific practices that have no scientific basis. Critics claim that the term is used as a weapon to attack innovation

(Sir) Cyril Burt. Burt was famous for research into the heritability of intelligence. He influenced other psychologists' work and was referred to as the 'father of the 11+ ', a selection examination that affected children's educational prospects. Burt invented data to suit his beliefs and was stripped of his knighthood.

TOPIC 10 — Psychology in action

The Chinese pseudoscience debate. There is an ongoing debate in China about traditional practices and philosophies labelled as pseudoscience. This is centred on China's Science Popularisation Law (2003), over which television debates and lawsuits have raged, with the scientific community claiming that because of widespread superstition in Chinese society, the public is hoodwinked by false scientific theories. There have even been calls for traditional Chinese medicines to be withdrawn from medical care, as they are not based on scientific principles.

However, Song (2006) claims that the refusal of the Chinese scientific community to accept controversial theories is due to conservative attitudes and narrow-mindedness.

Telepathy. This is a belief in communication through means other than the senses. Soal (1954) claimed evidence of telepathy with his subject Basil Shackleton. The evidence seemed credible and convinced a generation of researchers, until Markwick (1978) reanalysed the original results, finding that false data had been added.

Intelligent design. In 2005, a school board in Pennsylvania, USA, adopted a policy requiring science teachers to tell students that evolutionary theory is flawed and intelligent design is a valid alternative.

Intelligent design is an attempt by fundamental Christians to make the biblical story of creation seem scientifically credible. However, it is not supported by evidence, is invalid as a scientific theory and attacks the scientifically credible theory of evolution by spurious arguments and false accusations. Legal avenues have been used to legitimise intelligent design and destroy the credence of evolution.

Behe (1996) claims that there are complex systems unexplainable by evolution and that the universe is so unimaginably complex and perfect that it must have been created by an intelligent designer, opposing the accepted evolutionary idea of natural selection. Behe argues that evolution is scientific fraud because it cannot explain the evolution of the eye. However, computers running simulated evolution programmes have shown that evolution can explain the evolution of the eye as occurring in stages in which the function of the system changed.

Benna (2005) argues that intelligent design is an attempt by religious fundamentalists to destroy modern science, which it sees as an attack on morality and the Church itself.

Song (2006) believes that if the scientific community labels as pseudoscience theories that it does not know or understand, then science will be restrained from making innovations and scientific progress.

Fang Shimin (2006), head of China's 'scientific police', who consistently exposed examples of Chinese pseudoscience, was ruled by a court of law to have libelled Liu Zihua, who claimed to have used the 'Eight Diagrams Theory', based on the ancient Chinese philosophy of Bagua, to find a tenth planet in the solar system. This shows how pseudosciences persists if it attracts popular support and has traditional status and legal backing.

Ren (2007) believes that science should not be based solely upon repeatable experiments. However, Zhao argues that science is not over-conservative, but only accepts theories offering persuasive evidence.

Gilchrist (1997), a member of the National Centre for Science Education, assessed all peer-reviewed scientific journals published since intelligent design was first proposed, finding no articles supporting it, although he found thousands supporting evolution.

- Pseudoscience dresses itself up in scientific terminology and mirrors scientific practice because it wishes to acquire the high status and acceptability that science holds in society.
- It is important to have a demarcation between science and pseudoscience, as the acceptance of pseudoscientific beliefs and practices could lead to inefficient and dangerous practices in health care, environmental policy, science education and courts of law.

Q Describe issues of pseudoscience and/or scientific fraud. *(9 marks)*

Controversies relating to Ganzfeld studies of ESP and studies of psychokinesis

Ganzfeld studies. Metzger introduced the Ganzfeld (entire field) technique in the 1930s. The technique uses unpatterned sensory stimulation to produce an effect similar to sensory deprivation. Honorton (1974) developed the technique to assess extra-sensory perception (ESP) and it is now the main tool of parapsychological research.

In a Ganzfeld study, a receiver relaxes in a room for half an hour with halved table-tennis balls on their eyes, receiving white noise through headphones, creating a mild sense of sensory deprivation. A *sender* tries to communicate mentally a randomly chosen object, with the receiver describing mental communications that they feel they have received. During the judging procedure, the receiver, now out of the Ganzfeld state, has four possible targets, choosing the one best fitting the images experienced and therefore should get 25% correct. Some claim results gained go beyond this figure, but critics claim that evidence is inconclusive and cannot be taken as proof for the existence of ESP.

Hyman and Honorton (1985) produced independent meta-analyses of Ganzfeld data. Honorton claimed support for ESP, but Hyman did not, claiming that the experimental procedures were not rigorous enough or statistically analysed correctly, stating flaws in randomisation of targets and the judging procedure, as well as insufficient documentation. Honorton claimed that Hyman assessed too little data to perform proper factor analysis.

Hyman and Honorton (1986) issued a joint communiqué agreeing that the results were not due to chance or biased reporting, and agreeing a need for replication performed under more stringent conditions. Honorton then conducted autoganzfeld experiments, performed with computer control tests and the receiver isolated in a sound-proof, steel-walled, electromagnetically shielded room, reporting a statistically significant 34% accuracy rate.

- There is a danger of demand characteristics with the Ganzfeld technique, with believers in paranormal experiences producing seemingly correct answers. Results from Ganzfeld studies tend to match the beliefs of the researcher.
- Hyman (1995) claims that results will remain meaningless until an explanation of the process behind them is outlined and validated.
- The use of the Ganzfeld technique has led to the introduction of more rigorously controlled, unbiased research techniques.

Studies of psychokinesis. Psychokinesis (PK) is the process of moving or affecting physical objects by the mind, with no physical contact. The most famous practitioner is Uri Geller, a celebrity who supposedly uses PK to bend spoons. This is an example of *macro-PK*, which has a large effect, with *micro-PK* involving small effects on systems of probability, such as throwing dice. Claims have been made by psychics for levitation, moving objects and controlling weather patterns.

Benson et al. (2006) asked groups of Christians to pray for heart bypass surgery patients, with a control group of similar patients who were not prayed for. They found no significant differences in recovery rates; indeed, the prayed-for group had more complications. This suggests that prayer has no effect, although members of the control group may have been prayed for by friends and family.

Schmidt (1970) asked participants to observe a circle of nine lamps and, when one was lit, to try to move it mentally in a certain direction. Some participants were able to exert an influence, suggesting support for the existence of PK.

- There is a misconception that, if a researcher is testing paranormal ability, they must be measuring it. This is not necessarily true; they may merely be measuring the difference between chance predictions and actual outcome, with a bias towards the existence of PK emerging, as studies not finding significant results are not published.

- Radin (1997) believes that the insular nature of scientific disciplines hinders the acceptance of PK by other scientists.
- Magicians such as Randi have demonstrated the skills required for psychic processes, implying that other more natural processes are operating. They argue that if PK exists, why is it not used for human good rather than merely bending spoons, etc?

Q Outline Ganzfeld studies relating to ESP. *(5 marks)*

2 *Factors underlying anomalous experience*

Cognitive, personality and biological factors

Cognitive factors

Cognitive neuropsychiatry. This attempts to explain paranormal experiences by reference to models of cognitive functioning. The Cardiff Anomalous Perception Scale (CAPS), a 32-item self-reporting scale derived from anomalous literature, is used as a measuring tool, covering a range of sensory modalities, such as proprioception and time perception.

Cognitive illusions. People seek reasons for all experiences and cannot accept unexplained ones as random, meaningless occurrences.

Intuitive versus analytical thinking styles. Intuitive thinking styles have a tendency towards paranormal beliefs, while some studies find analytical thinking more associated with the paranormal. Other research has concentrated on intelligence levels and belief in the paranormal, with inconclusive results.

> **Brugger et al. (1993)** found participants viewing 'visual noise' pictures more likely to 'see' meaningful information if they believed in ESP, indicating that suggestibility is important.
>
> **Brugger et al. (1990)** found non-believers better at generating random numbers than believers, suggesting that they are more cognitively able.
>
> **Aarnio and Lindeman (2005)** found that women are associated more with paranormal beliefs, as they use intuitive thinking styles.
>
> **Wolfradt et al. (1999)** found contradictory results, with believers in the paranormal tending towards analytical thinking styles.

- Tests have been developed accessing and measuring paranormal beliefs, but not all test items relate to paranormal experiences.
- Research into thinking styles has produced contradictory evidence. For example, while some studies found a connection between paranormal beliefs and intelligence, Aarnio and Lindeman (2005) found a low correlation with psychology and medical students, suggesting that specific thinking styles are not linked to belief in the paranormal.

Personality factors

Locus of control. Early research demonstrated a relationship between external locus of control and belief in the paranormal as giving an illusion of control. However, subsequent research using specific measuring tools showed a link between external locus of control and superstition, suggesting a belief in fate, and found that an internal locus of control was related to beliefs in ESP, suggesting control by willpower.

Magical thinking (MT). Magical thinking — the idea that irrational beliefs occur by wishing for them — is among the defined symptoms of some psychiatric disorders, such as schizotypal personality disorder.

Wolfradt (1997) reported a positive correlation between external locus of control and a belief in superstition and spiritualism.

Davies and Kirkby (1985) found a relationship between internal locus of control and a belief in ESP.

Eckblad and Chapman (1983) found that high scorers on magical thinking had a predisposition to psychosis.

Thalbourne (1981) found that believers in the paranormal scored high on extroversion. However, **Lester et al. (1987)** found no such relationship.

- Locus of control correlates with beliefs in ESP, with some aspects under internal control and others under external control.
- Rattet and Bursik (2000) suggest that the contradictory results found in research into extroversion are due to methodological issues, such as measurement limitations, imprecise operational definitions of what constitutes psychic beliefs and researcher bias.

Biological factors

Brain areas. Stimulation of the right temporal lobe is linked to paranormal experiences. Temporal epileptics have reported seizures resulting in paranormal phenomena.

Evolution. The persistence of paranormal beliefs over time and across cultures implies an adaptive value, maybe as a consequence of needing explanations for events, which is important to gain control over one's environment. Another possibility is that paranormal beliefs evolved, as they give a sense of security when faced with unexplainable occurrences.

Brain biochemistry. High levels of dopamine are found in those who regard coincidences as meaningful and see patterns in random images.

Henschen (1925) found that tumours in the temporal region are associated with visual hallucinations, suggesting a biological explanation.

Penfold (1955) used electrical stimulation of the temporal region to produce heavenly music, hallucinations and vivid recollections from memory.

Brugger et al. (2002) found that heightened brain dopamine levels, from giving participants L-dopa, increased the identification of jumbled-up images of faces and words as real, among non-believers in the paranormal.

- Jansen (1996) believes that an evolutionary reason for the development of paranormal experiences is that they protect the brain against oxygen starvation, creating an expanded sense of awareness and attachment, helpful in life-threatening situations.
- Blackmore and Cox (2008) suggest that the frightening and bizarre hallucinations experienced on awakening by sufferers of sleep paralysis explain the universal features of alien abductions.

Q Discuss two factors underlying anomalous experience. *(25 marks)*

Functions of paranormal and related beliefs

Evolutionary. Paranormal experiences offer protection in threatening situations (see earlier).

Coping mechanism. Paranormal beliefs may serve as a psychological coping mechanism, with paranormal beliefs bringing a sense of reassurance in uncertain situations.

Dealing with uncertainty. Paranormal beliefs help people come to terms with situations of uncertainty that have no clear explanations.

Control. A belief in the paranormal provides individuals with a false sense of control.

Grieving. Paranormal beliefs allow grieving people to come to terms with their loss: for example, by talking to the departed in the spirit world.

Cultural significance. Paranormal beliefs serve to bind people together within a cultural grouping through shared belief systems, and represent culturally specific and culturally universal symbolism. Reality-defying beliefs are culturally universal, indicating a resistant, common function.

> **Watson et al. (2007)** found a relationship between children's loci of control and a belief in paranormal phenomena.
>
> **Irwin (1994)** found that children with an alcoholic parent had beliefs in witchcraft, superstitions and precognitions, suggesting that paranormal beliefs serve as a coping function.

- Blackmore (1997) thinks that believing in the paranormal provides a sense of certainty in those who have a poor understanding of probability.
- Irwin (2000) believes that theories of the functions of paranormal beliefs need to discriminate among different types of belief, as they may serve different functions.

Q Outline the functions of paranormal and related beliefs. *(9 marks)*

The psychology of deception and self-deception, superstition and coincidence

Deception. The accusation is that the paranormal is actually the product of deception by gifted practitioners. Lying and deception occur due to having a Theory of Mind, the ability to understand the mental state of others. Deception is also a part of Machiavellian intelligence, deliberately deceiving another for your own benefit. People are gullible for evolutionary reasons too, with humans having a need to connect invisible causes to events around them. Movement in the grass could be the wind or a predator — best then to presume it is a predator, suggesting that we are hardwired to assume there are agents controlling forces around us.

> **Swiss (2008)**, a magician and sceptic, demonstrated how telepathy, precognition, clairvoyance and psychokinesis are non-existent and the result of deceptive acts.
>
> **Shermer (2009)** found scientists susceptible to deception because they cannot comprehend others exploiting flaws.

- Pinker (2004) believes that paranormal beliefs bring deceivers the benefits of leadership and power.
- Some paranormal experiences may have explanations not related to deception, such as alien abductions being an effect of sleep paralysis.

Self-deception. The self-deception of scientists testing the paranormal may be due to their inability to comprehend flaws in their techniques and the desire of others to find and exploit them.

Self-deception can be *straight* self-deceiving, to believe something we want to be true (e.g. our loved ones live on in a spirit world), or *twisted* self-deceiving, to believe in something we wish not to be true (e.g. that monsters exist).

> **Gilovich (2009)** reports that we must be wary of tendencies to self-deceive by seeing patterns in random data, seeking confirmatory rather than disconfirmatory data, making biased evaluations of ambiguous or inconsistent data, and being uncritical of supportive data, while being critical of unsupportive data.

- Self-deception can be seen as a product of evolution, as it has a protective adaptive value.

Superstition. A superstition is an irrational belief that an object, action or circumstance, not logically related to a course of events, influences its outcome. It is often linked to magical thinking and ritual behaviours, if they are seen as magically affecting an outcome.

The motivation behind superstitions is a desire for control and certainty, with individuals searching for explanations of why things happen. The creation of false certainties is regarded as better than having no certainty at all.

Behaviourism explains superstitions through operant conditioning, either by positive reinforcement, where certain behaviours or objects become associated with pleasurable outcomes, or by negative reinforcement, where behaviours or objects become associated with reducing anxiety levels associated with uncertainty.

Skinner (1948) found that pigeons adopted body movement superstitions, learning to associate them with rewards of food pellets

Lustberg (2004) found superstitions among sportsfolk beneficial, as they increase confidence, motivation and persistence, enhancing chances of winning.

- Foxman (2009) believes that superstitions create expectations that can be powerful and suggestive, leading to biases to see them as true, but that they can have negative influences, by reinforcing maladaptive behaviours such as gambling.

Coincidence. A coincidence occurs when two unrelated events coincide. Although no obvious relationship exists, a belief forms, creating a cognitive bias that one causes the other. The perception of coincidences leads to occult or paranormal claims, supporting the belief system of fatalism, where events are seen as predestined. Coincidences also happen due to shortcuts in information processing, occurring as an attempt to simplify understanding.

Falk (1982) found that when extraordinary coincidences occur, people commit the error of singling that event out and according it significant status, suggesting a bias in cognitive processing.

- Chopra (2003) believes that the ancient Vedic philosophy that all events are related to unseen prior causes or associations, no matter how vast or trivial, and that therefore there is no such thing as coincidence, is becoming accepted by scientists.

Q Outline and evaluate the function of deception and superstition. *(20 marks)*

3 | *Belief in exceptional experience*

Psychic healing

Claims have been made for psychic healing powers, often by therapeutic touch, known as the 'laying on of hands'. Other claims are made for distance healing, where people are treated without physical contact, often over large distances. Charismatic religious figures are seen as possessing such a 'gift' and thus attain elevated status.

Psychic healers sometimes use mediums such as crystals supposedly to tap into bodily energy fields and sources, although much of the theory surrounding such ideas tends to be subjective and is not backed up with empirical evidence.

Grad (1959) studied Oskar Estabany, a cavalry officer with healing powers, finding that mice who had a portion of skin removed recovered faster if treated by Estabany. During his treatments, production of the enzyme trypsin was stimulated, suggesting a biological basis to psychic healing. Eskabany demonstrated his talent on humans, with **Krieger (1979)** finding that haemoglobin levels were stimulated during his treatments and stayed elevated for a year after, again implying a biological basis.

Braud and Schlitz (1988) investigated distance healing, getting healers to focus on photographs of patients for 1-minute periods. Patients were unaware of this, ruling out the possibility of placebo or suggestive effects. During healing it was found that galvonic skin responses, associated with activity in the sympathetic nervous system, altered, suggesting a biological influence.

- Mollica (2005) suggests that psychic healers are beneficial in dealing with widespread traumas occurring during catastrophes. After the Asian tsunami, patients treated by culturally familiar methods, such as psychic healing, often benefited more than those receiving medical treatments because they were offering 'psychological first aid' that is not intrusive or anxiety creating.
- The suspicion exists that many studies have not been rigorously controlled and therefore experimenter effects and demand characteristics have occurred. Therefore, more stringent studies are required, especially replications of earlier studies.

Out-of-body and near-death experiences

Out-of-body experiences (OBEs) is a term developed as a more bias-free label than others, such as 'astral projection' or 'spirit walking', and generally involves a feeling of floating outside your body, or even being able to see your own body from an exterior place.

There are *parasomatic* OBEs, where an individual has a body other than their usual one, and *asomatic* OBEs, where an individual feels they have no body. A rare type occurs when an individual feels there is a connecting cord between bodies.

The majority of OBEs occur in bed, suggesting a link to sleep and dream states, and also occur due to use of drugs such as ketamine.

Some people experiencing OBEs believe it was something they willed themselves, while others report sensations of being pulled involuntarily from their bodies, usually after a feeling of general paralysis. This suggests that OBEs may occur during a borderline stage between REM sleep and arousal when sleep paralysis occurs and dream images mix with usual sensory input.

OBEs can be encountered by people having dangerous near-death experiences (NDEs).

Blanke et al. (2005) found that OBEs were simulated in participants with no history of OBEs, by electrical stimulation of the right temporal-parietal brain area, suggesting a biological explanation.

Irwin (1985) reports that OBEs occur with very low or high arousal. **Green (1968)** found that 75% of participants experiencing OBEs had very low arousal, as they were lying down when the episode occurred, while a minority of cases happened during high arousal, such as in childbirth.

Ehrsson et al. (2007) used virtual reality goggles to con the brain into thinking the body was located elsewhere. Participants' bodies were then touched and the visual illusion, plus the feel of their real bodies being touched, made volunteers sense that they had moved outside their bodies. This suggests that OBEs may be triggered by a mismatch between visual and tactile signals.

- One possible practical application of research into OBEs is creating video games that give a sense of high levels of reality. It may also be possible for surgeons to operate on people long distances away, by controlling a robotic, virtual self.
- Entering a tunnel is a common occurrence with OBEs, and tunnel-like experiences also occur with epilepsy, falling asleep, meditation and some drugs, suggesting that the experience may be understood by reference to brain structures.

- Blackmore (1991) believes that NDEs provide no evidence for life after death, and are best understand by reference to neurochemistry, physiology and psychology.

Psychic mediumship

Mediums claim to have special powers allowing them to communicate messages from the afterlife, and they help people come to terms with the death of loved ones. There are two general sub-types:

Physical mediums. Physical phenomena are demonstrated that are viewable by an audience. Spirit people communicate to the living by raps, audible figures and materialised figures.

Mental mediums. Mental phenomena are demonstrated through the mind of a medium. This can occur in four ways:
- *clairvoyance* (where a medium sees a spirit)
- *clairaudience* (where a medium hears a spirit)
- *clairsentience* (where a medium senses the presence and thoughts of a spirit
- *trance mediumship* (where a medium is overshadowed by a spirit communicator speaking directly through the medium)

Schwartz et al. (2001) had five mediums interview a woman experiencing six significant losses in the last decade. The woman only answered 'yes' or 'no' to questions, to cut down on the chances of the mediums using intuitive reasoning. The mediums performed at an accuracy level of 83%, compared to 36% for control interviewers, suggesting a real psychic effect.

Rock et al. (2008) asked eight psychic mediums to describe independently how they experience receiving information from a discarnate (a deceased loved one) and seven common themes were found:

- multi-modal sensory impressions concerning the discarnate

- visual images of the incarnate in the medium's 'mind's eye'

- 'hearing' information from the discarnate in the medium's 'mind's ear'

- 'feeling' the discarnate's illness/cause of death

- experiencing aromas associated with the discarnate

- empathy with the discarnate

- alteration of mood while in contact with the discarnate

- Research into psychic mediumship especially raises ethical concerns, as those involved may be grieving for loved ones, and therefore procedures should be applied to eliminate any possibility of harm.
- Keen (1976), a well-known American medium, confessed to defrauding the public and detailed the techniques used by mediums to fool people into thinking they could conjure up spirits. Such techniques have been used by professional magicians to produce the same effects.
- Kelly (2008) believes mediums are not intentional frauds, but exploit vulnerable people emotionally. She believes that psychic mediumship concerns empathetic intuition or 'cold reading', where mediums tell people seemingly amazing facts they could only know by psychic methods, but which actually just misuse statistical probability to make them seem plausible.
- There may be a biased tendency to focus on events/facts from mediums that are true, and to ignore those that are not.

Q **(a)** Outline research into psychic healing.   *(5 marks)*
     (b) Outline and evaluate research into psychic mediumship.   *(20 marks)*

A The application of scientific method in psychology

1 *The main features of science*

Science is an objective, verifiable system of acquiring knowledge. The scientific method has four parts to it:

- observation and description of a phenomenon
- formulation of a hypothesis to explain the phenomenon
- use of the hypothesis to predict the existence of other phenomena, or to predict quantitatively the results of new observations
- performance of experimental tests of the predictions by several independent experimenters and properly performed experiments

Science is dependent on *empirical methods* of observation and investigation. This involves observations based upon sensory experiences rather than thoughts and beliefs. A scientific idea is one that has been subjected to empirical testing by the use of rigorous observations of events and/or phenomena. For science to make sense, there must be an explanation of empirically observed phenomena and this is achieved by developing theories that can be tested and improved by empiricism.

Science involves making predictions, tested by scientific observations made without bias or expectation by the researcher, and performed under controlled conditions. Theories and hypotheses are validated (found to be true) or falsified (found to be untrue) and it is the belief that this ability to predict and control behaviour under experimental conditions can also be achieved in real-life settings which makes psychology opt for science as its selected path towards acquiring knowledge.

Replicability. This involves repeating research under the same conditions. Research must be fully written up so that it can be properly replicated and its reliability and validity can be established. Fleischmann and Pons (1989) claimed to have created cold fusion, a form of low-energy nuclear reaction, in the laboratory, raising hopes of abundant, cheap energy. However, enthusiasm dropped when replications failed to get similar results. They either witnessed a separate phenomenon, or made errors in their procedures. Only by replication were scientists able to arrive at this conclusion.

Objectivity. Scientific research should be objective, perceived without distortion of personal feelings or interpretation. Objectivity is an integral part of empiricism, where observations are made through sensory experience and not from researchers' biased viewpoints. Such bias is often unintentional: for example, results from Ganzfeld studies, testing for the existence of ESP, tend to match the beliefs of individual researchers.

Cyril Burt was famous for his work on the heredity of intelligence, leading to the formation of the 11+ school entry examination, which affected many people's educational opportunities. However, Burt's research was deliberately faked to match his biased, subjective views about intelligence. Therefore due to a lack of objectivity, false findings occurred, leading to flawed practical applications.

Falsification. Part of the validation process is falsifiability, where a theory/hypothesis can be found to be false. Replication of research is the accepted manner of determining this.

The Chinese pseudoscience debate centres on the acceptance or not of so-called scientific theories based upon traditional Chinese philosophies, which are irrefutable: that is to say, they cannot be replicated and therefore validated or falsified. Some in China even argue for the banning of traditional medicines on the basis that they have not been scientifically validated.

2 *The scientific process*

Popper (1935) proposed the *hypothetico-deductive model* and advanced empirical falsification into scientific methods and procedures. He argued that, no matter how many positive validations of a theory occur, it does not prove it undeniably true. However, one example of falsification renders a theory untrue. Therefore, although we can disprove a theory, we can never be certain that it is irrefutably true.

Popper sees falsifiability as the determining line between what is and is not scientific. He attacked psychoanalysis as being unscientific because it is unfalsifiable.

Popper proposes *tentative theories* as the first stage in the scientific process. These generate *hypotheses*, which are tested by rigorous experimental means. Initial observations yield information about the world, formulated into theories that try to account for this information. Testing produces data that are statistically analysed to see if the theory can be refuted or falsified, often leading to adjustments in the theory. This is the process of *verisimilitude*, increasingly gaining closeness to the truth.

The scientific method operates as a cycle with set phases:
- *Inductive phase* — observations yield information used to formulate theories as explanations.
- *Deductive phase* — predictions are made from theories in the form of hypotheses, which are tested, yielding data that are analysed, leading to theory adjustment.

It then becomes possible to generate laws and scientific principles.

The chosen method of investigation is the *laboratory-based experiment*, which permits control over extraneous variables, with any change in the dependent variable being perceived as being due to manipulation of the independent variable. In this way, *causality* (cause-and-effect relationships) can be established.

Other methods of hypothesis testing have reduced ability to determine causality, such as *field* and *natural* experiments, but non-experimental methods can also be performed using the scientific method, such as *naturalistic observations*. Using methods such as inter-observer reliability, where researchers ensure that phenomena are observed in identical, unbiased ways, increases objectivity. Results are then seen as valid.

Psychology is often regarded as a 'soft science' because, due to the subjective subject matter, research is not carried out with total scientific vigour.

Kuhn (1962) argued that Popper's method of induction and deduction was not a true representation of how science works. He believed that scientists collect data fitting the accepted assumptions of a science, creating a type of bias whereby scientists attempt to find examples confirming their hypotheses rather than refuting them, with scientific journals publishing and focusing upon confirmatory examples of research, rather than non-confirmatory ones.

Kuhn called this a *paradigm*, 'a shared set of assumptions about the subject matter of a discipline and the methods appropriate to its study'. Eventually a paradigm is overthrown or rejected and replaced with a different, new paradigm, often emerging from a minority position: for example, the acceptance in physics of Einstein's beliefs.

Kuhn argues that scientific advancement occurs not through the steady progress advocated by Popper, but by revolutionary paradigm shifts.

It may be that psychology is not in its scientific phase, as it has yet to establish its paradigm. The counterview is that psychology has a number of paradigms, such as behaviourism and evolutionary psychology.

3 Validating new knowledge and the role of peer review

Part of the scientific verification process is peer review, which is considered fundamental to scholarly communication. It is used by scientists to determine whether research findings should be published. Peer review subjects research to independent expert scrutiny before it is decided whether to make it public.

Peer review is a security system reducing the chances of flawed or unscientific research being accepted as fact. The system operates on the belief that the status of research results is as important as the findings themselves.

Scientific developments are often the subject of news headlines, and a growing amount of scientific information is made public, as well as there being a growing number of organisations promoting and discussing scientific research, such as drug companies. Therefore it is difficult to decide which research is worthy of consideration and which is spurious, especially when scientists argue completely different viewpoints.

During peer review, it is normal for expert reviewers to be sent copies of a researcher's work by a journal editor. These reviewers report, highlighting any weaknesses and offering suggestions for improvement. There are four options for the reviewers to recommend:
- accept the work unconditionally
- accept it as long as it is improved in certain ways
- reject it, but suggest revisions and a resubmission
- reject it outright

Critics argue that peer review is not unbiased. Research occurs in a narrow social world and social relationships within that world affect objectivity and impartiality. In obscure research areas, it may not be possible to find experts to carry out a proper peer review. There have been accusations that some scientists' ability to consider research in an unbiased and professional manner is compromised by their being funded by organisations with interests in certain research being deemed scientifically acceptable. One way of addressing this is to ensure that reviewers are anonymous and independent.

Peer review is a slow process, sometimes taking years, and there may be resistance to revolutionary ideas that go against the elite or prevailing views, fitting Kuhn's idea of science not advancing steadily, but advancing by paradigms being toppled and replaced.

The consequences of false or unscientific research being accepted as true are serious because other scientists' research may be built upon the original research being true. Cyril Burt, who falsified research into the heritability of intelligence, was a major figure in the field. His research findings, accepted by psychologists as being valid, greatly influenced subsequent researchers, who took his work as a starting point for their own.

B Designing psychological investigations

1 Selection and application of appropriate research methods

Each research method has advantages and disadvantages and suits different situations.

Experiments. These are the most scientific form of research and the only method establishing causality. The laboratory experiment is the preferred type, allowing for strict control over variables, with field and natural experiments occurring in more natural circumstances, but with reduced control.

Field experiments use artificially induced independent variables, whereas natural experiments use naturally occurring ones.

Correlations. These show direction and intensity of relationships, but cannot establish causality or investigate non-linear associations. Correlations can be used when experiments would be unethical and to identify areas worthy of further investigation.

Self-reports. Questionnaires, interviews and surveys gain information from participants about themselves. A lot of data is gained in a relatively short period, although causality cannot be established and there are risks of idealised and socially desirable answers. Self-reports can identify areas worthy of further research by more stringent means. Interviews, unlike questionnaires and surveys, require face-to-face scenarios.

Observations. These are conducted when the emphasis is on seeing natural behaviour in a natural environment (though they can be conducted under laboratory conditions too). Causality cannot be established, and replication is difficult, but ecological validity is high.

Longitudinal studies. These are conducted over a long time period, usually at set intervals, where trends (changes over time) are considered. Causality cannot be established and *atypical sample attrition* occurs, where participants of a certain type drop out, biasing the sample.

Case studies. These are conducted on one person, or a small group, often to assess unique circumstances or find the source of a problem. They provide rich, detailed data, but their findings cannot be generalised, nor can they establish causality

2 Implications of sampling strategies

A sample is part of a target population used for research purposes. The idea is that what is true for a sample is true for the population that the sample represents. Several sampling methods are used, each entailing implications for bias and generalisation.

Random sampling. This occurs when members of a target population are selected without bias such as by drawing names out of a hat, or the use of random number tables, etc. Truly random samples are difficult to obtain, as all members of a target population are not generally available for selection. Random samples are not necessarily representative: random selection could theoretically produce a biased sample (e.g. all females), making generalisation difficult.

Opportunity sampling. This is popular, as the sample is easy to obtain, use being made of people's availability. Opportunity samples are often biased, as those available may be unrepresentative (e.g. all shoppers), again making generalisation difficult.

Self-selected (volunteer) sampling. The sample is generally obtained by advertisements or posters, requiring little effort. However, volunteers tend to be a certain personality type and therefore unrepresentative. They are often keen to help and therefore more at risk of demand characteristics.

Systematic sampling. Here the sample is obtained by selecting every *n*th person: for example, every fifth one. It is unbiased, producing fairly representative samples.

Stratified sampling. This involves selecting participants in proportion to their frequency in the target population. Individuals for each group (stratum) are randomly selected to produce a representative sample. If random sampling is not used for the strata, it is known as quota sampling.

3 Issues of reliability

Reliability refers to consistency. *Internal reliability* concerns the extent to which something is consistent within itself: for example, if all components of a test measure the same thing. *External reliability* concerns the extent to which a measure of something is consistent with other measures of the same thing.

If research findings are replicated consistently, they are said to be reliable. There are several ways in which reliability can be assessed and improved.

Inter-observer (rater) reliability. This concerns the extent to which there is agreement between different observers. If two observers agree on types of play in which children are involved, they have inter-observer reliability, but if they disagree, they do not have inter-observer reliability. Observers should agree *operational definitions* of the key categories being observed.

Split-half method. This assesses the extent to which individual items in a test or questionnaire are consistent with each other. The method involves splitting the test or questionnaire into two halves after data have been obtained: for example, comparing results from the odd questions with the even questions. If the results from the two halves correlate highly, then they are reliable; if not, the test needs revising.

Kuder–Richardson method. This concerns all the possible ways in which tests can be split in half and is a very rigorous method of assessing reliability.

Test–retest. This measures the stability of a test or interview etc. over time. It involves giving the same test to the same participants on two occasions. If identical results are obtained, reliability is established.

Reliability is important in itself, but also because validity cannot be established without reliability being established first. However, reliability does not guarantee validity.

4   *Assessing and improving validity*

Validity concerns accuracy, the degree to which something measures what it claims to. Validity refers to the legitimacy of studies and the extent to which findings can be generalised beyond the research setting as a consequence of a study's internal and external validity.

Internal validity. This concerns the extent to which the observed effect is attributable to the experimental manipulation (the influence of the independent variable on the dependent variable) and not some other factor: in other words, that it is measuring what it claims to. It could be argued that Milgram's electric shock study was internally valid, as participants believed it to be real.

External validity. This concerns the extent to which an experimental effect can be generalised to other settings (*ecological validity*), other people (*population validity*) and over time (*historical validity*). It could be argued that Milgram's electric shock study lacked external validity, as it is not a usual occurrence to shock people for getting questions wrong, it only used male participants and it was a product of its time.

Face (content) validity. This is a simple way of assessing validity, involving the extent to which items look like what the test claims to measure.

Concurrent validity. This assesses validity by correlating scores on a test with another test which is known to be valid.

Predictive validity. This is similar to concurrent validity, but the two sets of scores are obtained at differing points in time. For instance, the test should allow accurate predictions of future behaviour.

5   *Ethical considerations in design and conduct of psychological research*

Participants should be protected from harm and their dignity should remain intact.

If research is unethical, psychology will not have a respectable profile and people will be reluctant to participate, meaning that the subject will not advance or be of positive use. Ethical guidelines are in place to stop this occurring.

Informed consent. Participants are given all the details of the research, so that they can make a considered decision about whether to participate. Informed consent is gained from parents or legal guardians of those who are below the age of 16 or incapable of giving informed consent.

Presumptive consent. This is a means of getting informed consent from non-participants. People similar to those who will participate are given full details and asked if they would consent. If they agree, it is presumed to be ethical to perform the research.

Prior general consent. This performs the same function as presumptive consent, but participants agree not to be informed: that is, they agree to be deceived, but without knowing how or when.

Right to withdraw. Participants can withdraw at any point. No attempts should be made to persuade people to continue.

No deceit. Participants should not be deceived. Informed consent is not possible where deceit occurs.

Protection from harm. Participants should leave an experiment in the same physical and psychological state in which they entered it. No research should subject participants to levels of risk outside of those they would normally encounter. There is a debate as to whether this principle extends to animals too. Debriefings help to reduce the risk of harm. If unexpected harm occurs, it is the responsibility of the investigator to attend to it: for example, by providing counselling, etc.

No inducement to take part. Participants should not receive inducements to take part in research. The ability to decide whether to give informed consent is compromised by inducements to participate.

Confidentiality/anonymity. These are two related considerations. Details of participants' identities and performances should not be made public. Participants must consent to uses to which research findings will be put before research commences.

Ethical committees. These are comprised of experts in the field and concerned bodies, who consider all facets of the research and decide whether it is ethical and can proceed.

Cost–benefit analysis. This compares potential costs against benefits to decide if research should proceed. If benefits exceed costs, a decision to proceed can be taken.

Observations. These should only be conducted in circumstances where people would expect to be observed.

C Data analysis and reporting on investigations

1 *Appropriate selection of graphical representations*

Graphs display data in pictorial fashion, permitting an easily understandable alternative to numerical presentations. There are several types of graph, each used in different circumstances. Graphs should be titled and each axis, horizontal (x) and vertical (y), should be labelled. The vertical axis usually represents the dependent variable (frequency).

Bar charts. The height of the bar represents frequency. Bar charts differ from histograms (see below) in that empty categories are excluded. There is no true zero and data on the horizontal axis are not continuous. Bar charts can be used with words and numbers.

Histograms. These are similar to bar charts, but the area within the bars is proportional to the frequencies represented, the horizontal axis is continuous and there are no gaps between the bars.

Frequency polygon. This alternative graph to the histogram is used when two or more frequency distributions are compared on the same graph. The frequency polygon is drawn by linking the mid-points from the top of each bar in a histogram.

Scattergram. This is a type of graph allowing representation of the degree of correlation (similarity) between two co-variables. Scattergrams can display negative and positive correlations.

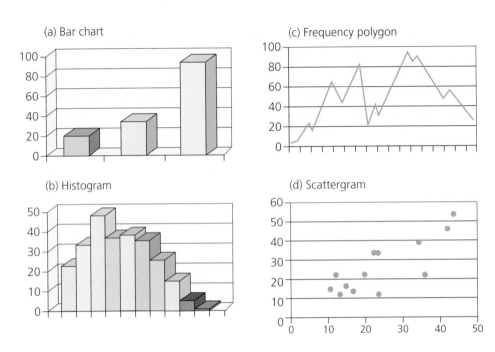

Figure 11.1 Displaying data graphically

2 Probability and significance

Research looks for differences or relationships between sets of data, particularly whether such differences and relationships are *significant* ones, beyond the boundaries of chance. The concept of probability is used to determine the cut-off point between two sets of data being significant or insignificant.

Probability concerns the degree of certainty that observed differences or relationships between two sets of data are real differences/relationships, or have occurred by chance. There is never a 100% certainty that differences and relationships are real ones — that is, beyond the boundaries of chance — so an accepted cut-off point is needed and a significance (probability) level of $p \leq 0.05$ is used. This means that there is a 5% possibility that an observed difference or relationship between two sets of data is actually not a real difference, but has occurred by chance, and this is seen as an acceptable level of error.

Sometimes stricter, more stringent levels of significance are needed: for example, if testing untried drugs or new research areas. Then a significance level of $p \leq 0.01$ might be used, meaning we are 99% certain that observed differences/relationships are real ones, but there is still a 1% chance that it occurred due to chance. If an even stricter level of $p \leq 0.001$ is used, this means we are 99.9% sure that it is a real difference/relationship, but there is still a 0.1% chance that it occurred by chance.

Type 1 and Type 2 errors

Type 1 errors occur when differences/relationships are accepted as real — that is, beyond the boundaries of chance — and we are wrong because the significance level was too high. This means the null hypothesis was wrongly rejected. With a 5% significance level, this means that, on average, for every 100 significant differences/relationships found, 5 of them are wrongly accepted.

Type 2 errors occur when differences/relationships are accepted as insignificant — that is, not real differences/relationships — and we are wrong because the significance level was set too low (for example, 1%), meaning that the null hypothesis was wrongly rejected.

A 5% significance level is the accepted level, striking a balance between making type 1 and type 2 errors.

3 Factors affecting choice of statistical test

Appropriate statistical tests are needed to analyse data. Four statistical tests are referred to in the specification (see section 4) and criteria exist to determine which one to use.

Levels of data measurement

Nominal. Data occur as frequencies/categories (e.g. how many people prefer Pepsi or Coke).

Ordinal. Data occur as ranks (e.g. finishing places, 1st, 2nd, 3rd in a running race).

Ratio. Data occur as units of equal size, with a true zero point (e.g. inches on a ruler).

Interval. Data occur as units of equal size, using both positive and negative numbers.

Test of difference or of correlation

If a relationship is being investigated, Spearman's rho is used. If a difference is being sought, a Wilcoxon signed-matched ranks test, a Mann–Whitney test, or a chi-squared test is used.

Experimental design

If a repeated measures design is used, a Wilcoxon test is performed. (A matched-pairs design is a special kind of repeated measures design, so its use also leads to performing a Wilcoxon test.) If data are at least ordinal and samples are independent, a Mann–Whitney test is used. If the data are at least nominal and samples are independent, select the chi-squared test.

4 The use of inferential analysis

Inferential tests show how likely it is that patterns observed in sets of data occur by chance and whether it is possible to infer that the same patterns exist in the general population. There are four tests in the specification of which knowledge is required.

- A *chi-squared test* is used when a difference is predicted between two sets of data, which are of at least nominal level, and an independent measures design was used. Chi-squared is also used as a test of association.
- A *Mann–Whitney* test is used when a difference is predicted between two sets of data, which are of at least ordinal level, and an independent groups design was used.
- A *Wilcoxon signed-matched ranks test* is used when a difference is predicted between two sets of data, which are of at least ordinal level, and a repeated or matched pairs design was used.
- A *Spearman's rho test* is used when a relationship is predicted between two sets of data, which are of at least ordinal level, and the data are pairs of scores from the same person or event.

Statistical analysis produces an *observed* value, which is compared to a critical value to determine if the observed value is significant. Critical value tables are referenced, taking into consideration whether a hypothesis is directional or non-directional (one-tailed or two-tailed), the number of participants or participant pairs (N) used and what level of significance is being utilised. Mann–Whitney and Wilcoxon tests require observed values to be equal to or less than the critical value, in order to be accepted as significant. Chi-squared and Spearman's rho tests require observed values to be equal to or greater than critical values, to be accepted as significant.

5 *Analysis and interpretation of qualitative data*

Qualitative data are non-numerical, such as a narrative of an interview. Such data provide insight about feelings and thoughts that quantitative data cannot. When analysing such data, researchers look for underlying meanings, and this can be subjective, based on the researcher's own interpretation. Qualitative data can be changed into quantitative data by being converted into categories or themes, to allow objective analysis by statistical means. *Content analysis* involves counting frequencies of occurrences: for example, children's drawings of a Christmas tree and presents could count the number of presents and their sizes, worth, etc.

6 *Conventions of reporting on psychological investigations*

Research is published in respected academic journals after peer review. There is a conventional, accepted way of presenting research in set sections.

- The *abstract* provides a summary, entailing details of aim(s), hypotheses, participants, methods and procedures, findings and conclusions.
- The *introduction* presents a review of associated previous research. This has a logical progression into aims and hypotheses.
- The *method* section presents details of the method used, independent and dependent variables (or co-variables in the case of a correlation), controls, sampling details, ethical considerations, procedures, etc. — in short, all details necessary to permit exact replication. Tests/questionnaires etc. used are placed in the appendices, but are referred to here.
- The *results* section describes the results, comprising a summary of raw data and measures of central tendency and dispersion, in written form as well as in appropriate graphs and tables. Details are included of inferential statistical analysis, indicating whether results are significant. Actual raw data and statistical calculations are referred to here, but are placed in the appendices.
- The *discussion* section assesses findings in terms of previous research, outlines limitations, while suggesting possible modifications, proposes ideas for future research and outlines implications of the research.
- The *appendices* include raw data, questionnaires, calculations, references, materials used, etc.

Q A psychologist presented information to participants either via printed-paper (Group A) or displayed on a computer screen (Group B). Group A recalled 85% of the information and Group B 4%.

- **(a)** Write a suitable non-directional hypothesis for this investigation. *(2 marks)*
- **(b)** The investigation generated quantitative data. Give one advantage of this type of data. *(1 mark)*
- **(c)** A Mann–Whitney statistical test was used to analyse the data from this investigation. Give two reasons for using this statistical test. *(2 + 2 marks)*
- **(d)** Describe one conclusion that can be drawn from this investigation. *(2 marks)*
- **(e)** An opportunity sample was used in this investigation. Give one strength and one weakness of this sampling method. *(2 + 2 marks)*
- **(f)** The research was subjected to peer review before being published. Explain the role of peer review. *(10 marks)*
- **(g)** The psychologist noticed that older participants seemed to have more difficulty in operating computers than younger participants. Design a study to investigate possible age differences in operating computers. You should include sufficient details to permit replication: for example, a hypothesis, variables, details of design and procedure, and sampling. *(12 marks)*